CHRISTIANITY
beyond
CREEDS

*Making religion
believable for today
. . . and tomorrow*

BY HARRY T. COOK

The Center for Rational Christianity
Clawson, Michigan

For information, contact the Center For Rational Christianity, PO Box 182, Clawson, Michigan 48017.

Library of Congress Catalog Card Number: 97-077496

Cook, Harry T.
Christianity Beyond Creeds/ Harry T. Cook — 1st Ed.

ISBN 0-9660728-0-4 12.95

Designer: Susan M. Chevalier
Copy Editor: Emily M. Everett

Table of Contents

Preface i

Part One: Belief and Believing 1

Part Two: Practical Implications 41

Part Three: The Bible Without Creeds 78

A Personal Word 101

Appendix A: Unpacking Resurrection-Speak 108

Appendix B: What Jesus May Have Actually Said 113

Preface

In Willa Cather's *Death Comes for the Archbishop*, the prelate is depicted circa 1850 as pondering two pieces of Spanish-American-Indian lore which were commonly held explanations of why a certain tribe seemed to be dying out. The first had to do with a legendary fire that burned perpetually in a mountain cave. The service of the ceremonial fire was said to have sapped the strength of the best and the brightest of the tribe's young men — thus rendering them incapable of siring children on a dependable basis. The other was that members of the tribe regularly sacrificed infants to an enormous serpent that dwelt also in nearby mountains.

Cather has her archbishop observe that "it seemed much more likely that the contagious diseases brought by white men were the real cause of the shrinkage of the tribe." Cather's work, of course, is fiction, but her imaginary archbishop was certainly not the first cleric of his day to try to rationalize the causes of natural phenomena. Charles Darwin, deacon of the Church of England and epoch-making scientist, was another.

This book attempts to construe belief in Enlightenment terms that will make sense in the contemporary world in which the laws and theories of Newton, Copernicus, Galileo, Darwin, Freud and Einstein are held by most rational persons to be provisionally explanatory of why things are as they are.

The method will be to take the terms of the baptismal (or Apostles') creed, which are regularly confessed in the public worship of most Christians, and to examine and analyze each in light of what is commonly accepted about the nature of life in the known universe and then to restate them in language that is appropriate to contemporary thinking.

The purpose is to enable those who wish to continue in the tradition of Christianity to do so with intellectual integrity intact — much as Cather's archbishop looked at the same data at which that native tribe looked but came up with a rational explanation for their existence.

A second section will explore what congregational life might look like in a Christianity beyond creeds. In a concluding section, several scriptural texts will be analyzed along the same lines in an effort to show that such texts are as available to rational interpretation as to dogmatic construction. An appendix analyzing resurrection texts is offered together with a second appendix which is a fresh translation of New Testament sayings that can reasonably be attributed to Jesus. It is my desire that this work be approached with an open mind by any who may encounter it and used as a foil in the re-examination of the terms of traditional beliefs.

— Harry T. Cook

Part One:
Belief and Believing

I

The world of belief can be contradictory and often irrational. A general rule of thumb might be that a particular belief or even an entire belief system becomes important to defend because it serves some emotional, societal or economic self-interest of the believer. I take myself as an example. When I allow myself to contemplate the universe absent an orderer or, at the very least, an organizing principle, I become upset and anxious. The progress of modern astrophysics which I follow from an avid amateur's distance posits a universe of many billions of years in age with anomalies right and left, as well as much that is predictable and dependable. Many an astrophysicist is willing to leave the data as is, unexplained as to origin or originator — mostly, I suppose, because no data exist that might suggest one or the other. I find myself jumping over data gaps to posit an overarching intelligence that to my way of thinking must be responsible for the universe, if not omnipotent and omniscient. I find myself further willing to believe and, in fact, believing in the existence of such an intelligence. And because of my background as a Christian, I am provisionally content to use the term "god" in referring to it. Now I have framed a belief that serves an important self-interest.

Several male acquaintances of mine are firmly convinced that, in many important ways, women are inferior to men. They say, in fact, that they believe that proposition to be true. Thus have they formed a belief that serves their self-interest as males. Caucasian Americans in the Civil War South believed that Negroes were inferior to whites and that, therefore, slavery (cheap labor) was justified. They framed a belief that served their self-interest as slaveholders. The Nazis believed that Jews were not only inferior but subhuman. Millions of Christians believe Jesus of Nazareth was physically raised from the dead and that those who so believe will likewise be raised from the dead. It is clear what self-interests such beliefs serve.

Some self-interests are benign and some malign. But they have in common the overriding motivation to make data conform to wish or need. Proclamation that such and such a thing is objectively and absolutely true does not, of course, make it so. If intellectual integrity is a primary value, then it is important to ground belief in data and to be content with a lot of ambiguity and contradiction in doing so. I can say with the backing of centuries of observable data that "the sun rises in the east," and anyone would know what I mean and agree. Of course, the sun does no such thing. Rather it is Earth rotating on its axis that makes the sun appear to rise and set. But no matter how I say it, the belief is at least grounded in a datum: Something is moving. In other words, the interpretation of an observed datum can be faulty or mistaken even if the observation is properly made. So: "I believe that the sun rises in the east" is, as far as it goes, accurate because the body seems to be moving. But once it is discovered that the ground on which the observer stands is itself moving, then the same datum is better interpreted as, "Earth rotates on its axis and in so doing exposes progressively different areas of itself to the sun, making it seem as if the sun is moving." Now virtually anyone who has passed fourth-grade science knows and (one supposes) believes the latter statement to be true. But almost anyone would state it in the first way and would be understood as expressing what is so.

The question is: How can the language of Christian belief be construed so that the data which first gave rise to its expression can be examined in light of the worldview by which we now interpret natural phenomena? Then may come the eventual reconstruction of the belief system which could make it and its terms credible and usable to people in our time.

It is with that proposition in mind that I say the historic creeds of Christianity can no longer be used unexamined and without a new and responsible construction of their terms in Enlightenment language and concept. As they exist now and as they are commonly used, it is necessary to work around them. The worldviews they represent are of eras before Copernicus, Galileo, Newton, Darwin, Freud and Einstein, and all those intellectual giants have contributed to our 20th-century appreciation of the natural order. Our world is light years beyond those of the apostles, of Tertullian, Athanasius, Augustine, Aquinas, Luther and Calvin. New lenses are available through which we may perceive that world and our human part in it. If the Christian belief system is to survive as more than an artifact, if the centrality of Jesus is to mean anything beyond pious need-fulfillment, then our work is cut out for us. It is time to look with a critical eye at the creeds — anti-thought prisons in which the church confined itself willingly much too early in its life. In fact, if the church is to be preserved for useful and intellectually responsible work, it needs to become a Christianity beyond creeds — at least the creeds it now has.

Creeds are attempts to define what is orthodox and what is not. Creeds are attempts to delimit belief in certain terms and to exclude from a given fellowship those who do not profess such creeds or cannot profess every term of a given creed. If creeds could be thought of as temporary, "here's-where-we-are-now-or-were-then" statements and treated as open-ended and available to revision as those who continue to confess them come to new and different appreciation of what at first they believed, the creeds would be useful as points of reference — just as the light from stars long since extinct can be seen today and used as astronomical points of reference. But as they are and as they are commonly used, the major creeds of Christianity (the baptismal or Apostles' and the Nicene creeds) are most often treated as settled and their rationalization tolerated only to a limited degree.

The Apostles' Creed is not "apostolic" in the sense that the earliest followers of Jesus received it from him or even composed it themselves. All competent church historians date the baptismal creed from the second century C.E. The most conservative reading of its history would be that it contains witness passed on from the first to the second to the third generations of Christians. It soon enough became the baptismal creed as candidates were asked if they believed in God the Father, God the Son and God the Holy Spirit. With each affirmative answer, the candidate was immersed. (Pliny, in reporting to Trajan, said that he required one accused of being a Christian three oaths to that effect before he or she was taken to punishment — perhaps an adumbration of the threefold baptism.) In due course, the baptismal creed found its way into the regular liturgies of the church and is found today in the Anglican offices of Morning and Evening Prayer, and, after the example of antiquity, in the baptismal liturgy.

The Nicene Creed was a much more ambitious undertaking in a different era. In the early to mid-fourth century C.E., an attempt was made to unite the disparate factions of Constantine's empire.

Constantine looked around and saw the church everywhere. That, he determined, would become the glue that would tie it all together. He claimed that he had had a vision commensurate with that lofty aspiration and forthwith decreed that Christianity would be the state-sanctioned, official religion of the Empire. The edict was insufficient to stem the tide of dissension over such profound issues as whether the Son was begotten or made and whether he was of the same or of a similar substance as the Father. It took the fathers at Nicaea a good long while to work out the compromise that issued in the creed that bears the adjectival form of the name of the city in which the ecumenical council took place. After some expansion and revision in 381 in the Council of Constantinople, the church has confessed the Nicene Creed ever since. The Eastern and Western rites later parted company over the procession of the Holy Spirit — whether from the Father or from the Father and the Son. The Anglicans have waffled over both the double procession and whether it is "I" or "we" who believe. No revisions along those lines have rescued the document from its hopeless captivity to the fourth century and its worldview.

II

"I believe in God the Father Almighty..."

Belief in someone or something is ipso facto a highly subjective proposition. I believe on the basis of what my senses have told me countless times over the past 18 years that the woman to whom I am married exists. That is one thing. But I also believe *in* her, and that is something that has taken time and trust. I can explain to anyone why I believe she exists. But my belief in her existence is not its cause. My believing *in* her is likewise not the cause of her exemplary and loving character. It may be that another might not find her so exemplary and loving. I don't know. And I cannot suppose that all

5

people could or would believe *in* her. I cannot transfer my time with and trust in her to somebody else. And yet anyone who has ever encountered her would believe she exists, for she is visible, audible and palpable. Moreover, I could hardly have come to believe *in* her if she were not visible, audible and palpable. Yet, if I went around saying that I believed an invisible, inaudible and insubstantial person existed and, moreover, said I believed *in* him or her, I would rightly be diagnosed as delusional. How then can it be rational and credible to say "I believe in God" or that "God is." And why are people who profess such belief not considered delusional? Answer: because belief in a supernatural and powerful being or entity is socially acceptable and, truth to tell, often socially required. I may profess belief in Harvey, the invisible rabbit, but not without fear of being institutionalized. But I may profess belief in an invisible god. At least I know what Harvey is likely to resemble *if* he becomes visible. I haven't the slightest idea of what a god would look like.

To return to my own need-based belief in an orderer or organizing principle, I will say that the very existence of what sometimes appears to be both a vast and orderly universe suggests that some kind of planned or experimental order might underlie it. I would put forth as data the exquisitely measurable movements of the stars and planets, the emergent design of the human fetus, the harmonizations of Mozart, the complex relationships among biological species (including human beings) and the capacity of some human beings generously to care for one another in ways that bring order out of chaos. Both emotional need and reason (perhaps driven by that need) lead me to posit a life source and/or orderer that stands behind those observable phenomena. I am finally unwilling to use the word "god" as a term to account for such a source/orderer *unless* I can say I believe in that god in the same way I can reasonably say "the sun rises in the east." I do not wish to anthropomorphize or personalize that "god" or attribute to it more than should be attributed. My need begs to have me say that "god" is "almighty" in the same way I needed to think that my father, now of blessed memory, could and would do anything, never err or be less than perfect.

What are the data offered to suggest that a life source/orderer is "almighty"? Certainly if one is considering seriously the proposition that it may be responsible for the movements of the planets and for the ornate complexity of life in the biosphere, it might be rational to consider further that a source/orderer has plenty of power. Whether or not it is omnipotent is a question beyond the data at hand. Just so, there are plenty of data to suggest credibly that it is not "almighty." If one takes into consideration the imbalances and anomalies of nature as well as the evils that human beings perpetrate upon one another, there is ample reason to suggest that a source/orderer would be neither "almighty" nor even entirely benign. Natural phenomena — earthquakes, killer storms, climate irregularities, genetic anomalies and the like — are to one degree or another explainable. We know what causes earthquakes: It is the Earth itself still in the process of formation or devolution. We think we know what is causing some weather abnormalities — if indeed we know enough to say what is and what is not normal: It is the overuse of fossil fuels, chlorofluorocarbons and the burning of rain forests. We are only just beginning to plumb the vast mystery of genetics in an attempt to figure out fetal abnormalities. And we suppose they *are* abnormalities. If the source/orderer were omnipotent and the human suffering caused by nature as here described is part of human experience, then an "almighty" one could not at the same time be entirely benign.

In fact, we cannot know or even assume that a source/orderer might be "almighty." We can wish it were or weren't. But reason again demands that if one believes a source/orderer to be "almighty," then, given the terrible things that are visible to the eye, audible to the ear and corrosive of the biosphere and of the human spirit, one cannot at the same time believe that it is all good. The Genesis writer's image of Elohim brooding over the primordial chaos and wresting from it some semblance of order is probably closer to the credible truth of the matter than all the pious incantations about omnipotence. Can we not be content with saying that a source/orderer some like to call "God" may be engaged with forces that are not perhaps entirely under its control, and that order continues to appear out of the vortex of disorder, even as disorder sometimes seems to rule the day?

Elie Wiesel, a holocaust survivor, has looked into the abyss these kinds of questions inevitably raise. In his book of memoirs he wrote: "Auschwitz is conceivable neither with God nor without Him. Perhaps I may someday come to understand man's role in the mystery Auschwitz represents, but never God's" (*All Rivers Run to the Sea*, 1995, Alfred A. Knopf, p. 85). Wiesel refers to a midrash in which God is depicted as weeping over the disaster human beings have made of creation, then writes: "Perhaps God shed more tears in the time of Treblinka, Majdaneh and Auschwitz; one may therefore invoke His name not only with indignation but also with sadness and compassion."

One presumes that Wiesel, in speaking of God, is speaking of Jahweh, that desert deity encountered, it is said, by Abraham and later Moses and the generations of Semites who lived before and into the Common Era. Jahweh is an interesting projection of human need and fear upon the face of a mysterious universe. He is by turns powerful, petulant, calculating, vengeful, merciful and puzzling — that is, those are the ways in which he is depicted by various traditions throughout the pre-Common Era epoch. This should come as no surprise since Jahweh is often depicted as acting as those who profess belief in him wish him to act. The pre-exilic prophets all but demanded harsh judgment upon Israel and Judah. Jahweh is thus depicted as opening the door to the depredations, for example, of Nebuchadrezzar. Likewise the second Isaiah saw in Cyrus of Persia a secular savior but found cause to dub him Jahweh's "anointed." Why is it not as legitimate to imagine or even posit a source/orderer from historic as well as natural data? Let us say that it *is* as legitimate, but in saying so let us avoid what the philosopher Richard Rorty calls a "final vocabulary," as if the words we use to account for our hunches that certain natural phenomena or events and developments in history are actually descriptive of a source/orderer. The point is that theism has become increasingly unworkable as the implications of the Enlightenment and the advances of science have altered our operative worldview.

What might well be worth aiming for is a kind of atheism in which a source/orderer is considered as a distinct possibility and then to seek a metaphor that resonates well in these days. We cannot live in other days — past or future. We can, in fact must, live now, and if god-talk is to be a relevant and useful part of our lives it must be expressed and construed in terms that make sense. To posit an "almighty" god that micromanages nature and human affairs down to and including the fall of every sparrow and the counting of head hair is to engage in unreason and self-delusion. The same might be said of the "abba" with whom Jesus is depicted as conversing.

Only in a society that is patriarchal in nature or otherwise male-dominated is it likely that the perceived source/orderer will be depicted as "father." If the term is used simile-like to propose that it is "like" a father in that a father is the progenitor of life, the simile is still unworkable. The life we know best — human and animal — is of biological necessity the result of joint male and female activity. Fathers by themselves do not reproduce. Neither do mothers. Is it then possible or desirable to depict the supposed source/orderer as "parent?" Not really. Parents become parents only because they tap into powers resident in themselves by nature — powers inherent in their biology. The act of sexual intercourse is normally not a calculated task of inventors but an abandonment to passion with conception certainly an agendum of nature and even sometimes of those who have intercourse. Added to that obvious reality is the fact that parents are not necessarily good people. They are sometimes cruel and negligent, and even at their best they are individuals for whom childbearing and rearing are sometimes unwanted tasks. Each of us has seen in his or her father or mother unhappy and unfortunate traits, habits and actions. Even the most romanticized images of father or mother cannot realistically carry the day as icons of what many people want to believe about god.

So let us jettison the "father" and "parent" analogies as unworkable and unhelpful. Especially the male imagery. It stands to reason that any source/orderer of both male and female is either beyond or other than both. Thus, for the same reason, we set aside such verbal icons as "master," "lord" and "king." Perhaps the encounter Moses is said to have had with the desert deity has something to offer this discussion: Moses said to Elohim, "If I come to the Israelites and say to them, 'Elohim of your ancestors has sent me to you,' and they ask me 'What is his name (nature)?' what shall I say to them?" Elohim said to Moses, "I will be what I will be" (Exodus 3:13-14a). (Everett Fox in his translation renders it: "I will be-there howsoever I will be-there" (*The Five Books of Moses*, 1995 Schocken Books, p. 273).

The one difficulty with the first-person singular pronoun is that it suggests an objective personal entity engaged in human discourse. Even granting that "elohim" is plural and that the verse might have read "We will be-there howsoever we will be-there," the problem remains.

So what now do we do with "Credo in unum Deum" or with "I believe in God the Father Almighty"? If it is agreed that belief needs be grounded in observable or even "perceivable" data, then we must say, "I *need* to believe in a source/orderer I infer from my observations of nature and history. And I need to believe that to one degree or another that my inferred source/orderer is to one degree or another in charge of the universe and that it might be as kindly disposed to my well-being as a good parent ought to be for his or her offspring." Granted, the statement is prolix and lacks the poetic grandeur of the historic creeds. But it is honest and locates belief in the subjectivity of an intelligent and inquiring person who does not set his/her belief in concrete and then proceed to make an idol of it and to coerce others into confessing the belief because it is "correct." Yet once the need-based aspect of belief is acknowledged, a great many people who now uncritically profess orthodox Christian beliefs as their "final vocabulary" might well be comfortable with the proposed and provisional reconstruction of "I believe in God the Father Almighty."

"The sun rises in the east" is simple, straightforward, even poetic in an elementary way. But it is wrong. What is correct is: "Earth rotates on its axis and in doing so progressively exposes different areas of itself to the sun." Prolix, prosaic, but correct. "I believe in God the Father Almighty" is a statement of great resonance and power, but it is completely without grounding in what is and can be known. Conversely, "I need to believe in a source/orderer I infer from my observations of nature and history. And I need to believe that to one degree or another my inferred source/orderer is in charge of the universe and that it might be as kindly disposed to my well-being as a good parent ought to be for his or her offspring" does not lend itself to solemn intonation or chant, but it is at least honest.

III

"Maker of heaven and earth."

The Nicene Creed, as if for clarification, adds "of all things seen and unseen." We get the point. Maker of everything. "I made a cake," says the proud baker. He means that he took flour, baking pow-

11

der, eggs, shortening, salt and sugar — none of which he made — and put them into a bowl, stirring them into batter. He then poured the mixture into a pan and placed it in a heated oven — having done nothing but start a fire, put match to a gas jet or simply flip a switch. Thirty to 45 minutes later, voila!, a cake. He made a cake, or did he? What he did in actuality was, knowingly, to mix more or less precise amounts of the various necessary ingredients and submit them to a process already in place. It probably was a wonderful, a stupendous, utterly mouth-watering cake. But he did not "make" the cake. The Priestly writers told memorably of "a wind from Elohim" sweeping over the face of the primordial waters. From what follows in Genesis 1:3-31, it seems clear that the writer meant his or her readers to imagine Elohim moving to bring order from the "tohu wa bohu," or "the formless void and darkness" — or as Fox translates it: "wild and waste." In a rather trivial but still analogous way, the baker engaged in a similar process — bringing a useful order from disparate elements which by themselves make nothing. To the extent that the baker is seen as a catalyst in the process, one can say the baker is a maker.

Of a source/orderer it might credibly be said that it may in some way have appropriated or even originated the universe's energy if not its substance, and, on a trial-and-error basis, has been experimenting ever since. A deist would simply say the first domino was tapped and what's happened since has happened — as the memorable bumper sticker puts it in less genteel terms.

The work of astrophysicists and astronomers reveals an incomprehensibly enormous universe with new and distant galaxies being discovered and probed. Likewise microbiologists are exploring, rather than through telescopes, through microscopes. Each discipline discovers and probes apparent order and apparent disorder, even chaos. What generally is concluded is that most things are in flux, even if change and movement are sometimes minuscule and infrequent. Therefore it becomes rationally difficult to assert that the universe ("heaven and earth" and "all that is seen and unseen") has or had a "maker." Processes have been ongoing for aeons and aeons that have produced and are producing and presumably will continue to produce energy and matter in bewildering quantities and qualities that in and by themselves will alter the state and maybe even nature of the universe. It all has the earmarks of a vast experiment or process of trial, error and retrial. A source/orderer could in such a scenario be credibly imagined or posited as a command center through which stimuli, signals and directions might be sent and received, encoded and decoded and retransmitted.

The theories of evolution and relativity and the continued testing of them by scientists demand that we not be simplistic in pressing our need to believe in a god who made the universe. What Darwin and Einstein alone illuminated of the way certain processes may be working remains breathtaking in its scope and implication. "Make" is a fine and simple verb. But it cannot be used of the universe or any part of it. Something of unimaginable force and movement is now, and has been under way for time out of mind, yielding such rudimentary substances as salt, sugar, grain and water out of which, at least in part, someone can "make a cake." But even as he or she "makes" it, it is clear that nothing has been made but rather substances and processes have been employed in an intelligent way so as to yield the cake. I can then say, "God, Maker of Heaven and Earth" in the same way as I can say that I am making or have made a cake.

By saying "Heaven," though, "and Earth" — meaning all things seen and unseen — do we ask for trouble by attributing so much to a source/orderer? What about the chemical disorder in my sister's brain that has made most of her adult life a living hell as she copes with a bipolar personality? What about the malignant cell that one day burst its walls in my mother's stomach and, with its metastasizing fellows, took her life away inch by inch, month by agonizing month? What about the inchoate rage that caused Adolf Hitler, Pol Pot, Saddam Hussein and Ratko Mladic to become mass murderers? Such disorders surely could not have been made by a god who is perceived by needy human beings to be caring. The cruel explanation often given by non- or fuzzy thinkers is that "God has a purpose for everything." Better, though, to accept and deal with the ambiguity that such disorders introduce into one's picture of the universe. Something far, far beyond even the understanding of an Einstein is going on, and we experience what we take to be the good it produces as well as what we take to be the bad. Of any or all of that, it is not rational to attribute its deliberate origins or developments to a single, purposeful source or "maker."

IV

"Jesus Christ, his only Son, our Lord."

The one word in this clause of the creed that has any grounding in reality at all is "Jesus." Preachers, Sunday School teachers and catechists often speak of Jesus as if he were a historical character on par with Alexander the Great, Julius Caesar or, closer to our day, Thomas Jefferson. About these latter three, substantial attestation to their existence and accomplishments is extant. It can be said responsibly from a historian's viewpoint that they actually lived. Far, far less — again from a historian's viewpoint — can be reliably known about Jesus. The most reliable sources that indicate there was such a person are the Gospel of Thomas and the collection of sayings known as the "Quelle" — or source — which turn up in sometimes altered forms in the gospels of Matthew and Luke. Both Thomas and the Quelle consist in wisdom sayings and parables attributed to Jesus of Nazareth who appears to have been a peasant cynic-like sage who,

14

unlike his contemporary John the Baptist, seemed to have eschewed apocalypticism in favor of sapientialism, i.e., figuring out ways to make life work in the world as it was rather than renouncing the world and condemning it to imminent divine judgment. Hence, the wisdom sayings.

For the first roughly 20 to 25 years after the disappearance of Jesus from the scene, communities appear to have formed around those sayings, orally transmitting them and later writing them down, expanding and altering them to suit local and contemporary needs. (A useful analysis of this period is *The Last Gospel — The Book of Q & Christian Origins* by Burton L. Mack, 1993, HarperSan Francisco.) However, the sayings by themselves probably could not sustain such communities the further removed in time they became from the original speakers. Clearly by the time of Paul, the "sayings communities" that may have resembled synagogues had become part of a newer and different movement having taken on the trappings similar to a Greek mystery cult.

Mack writes: "The evidence from Paul's letters is that congregations of the Christ were attractive associations and their emerging mythology was found to be exciting" (Mack, p. 219).

One might guess that the ongoing conflict between Jesus and the Pharisees and between Jesus and "the Jews" depicted by the synoptic gospel writers and by John, respectively, is really a reflection of what Mack describes as the "freedom from cultural traditions and the personal experience of transcending social constraints." But there may have been a factor of much more profound significance that accounts for the passage of what he called "early Christianity" from the wisdom-saying communities to the full-blown Greek mystery cult. And that was the defining moment in the Jewish-Roman War as the Temple in Jerusalem was desecrated and destroyed in 70 C.E. That central shrine and historic point of reference and all that it meant even to those Jewish factions more at home with rabbinical Judaism was gone, and with it the profound sense of identity with a past. Perhaps the Jerusalem disaster rendered the Jesus communities, already in competition with rabbinical Judaism, unable to carry the day with only their collection of wisdom sayings as literature. Perhaps they set out to restore something of the "Temple" flavor to their lives by embracing the liturgical forms of the mystery cults. In doing so what may have happened is that the by-then historically remote and obscure Jesus was restored and transformed into a human-divine mythic figure, the son of the invisible god. Conflating the Jewish image of messiah with the "son of God," the new cultic communities imposed upon Jesus' death, the circumstances of which were almost assuredly by that time lost in obscurity, a new meaning, viz., of atonement. The salvation of members of the cult came through the death of the messiah-son and, particularly, by his blood that was not only shed but of which in the ritual meal they drank.

To get to that point, it was necessary to retrieve or to create "the story" of Jesus, to put some flesh on the bare bones of a sketchy portrait that could only be inferred from the sayings. The Gospel of Thomas contains only the sayings, its author evidently having found no cause to include biographical information that he may or may not have possessed. Paul seemed to know little of the sayings or any of the biographical details supplied later by the authors of the synoptic gospels and passed on to the language and spirit of the mystery cults (see Galatians 3:2-6; Colossians 1:15-22, 2:8-15, for example). It is worth mentioning, however, that there are interesting parallels between Romans 13:7, where Paul wrote: "Pay to all what is due them — taxes to whom taxes are due...," and Thomas 100 "Give Caesar what belongs to Caesar; give God what belongs to God" and Mark 12:17 "Give to the emperor the things that are the emperor's, and to God the things that are God's." Likewise, Paul states in Romans 14:14

"I know and am persuaded in the Lord Jesus that nothing is unclean in itself" and Mark's editorial comment in 7:19 is "Thus he declared all foods clean." This may suggest that Paul knew of some of the Jesus sayings. And Paul does take notice in I Corinthians 11: 23-26 of an event the synoptic gospels similarly depict. (See Mark 14: 22-25 and parallels in Matthew 26:26-29 and Luke 22:14-20.)

However, it was Mark who pulled the disparate elements of "the story" together and in so doing created a new literary form: the proclamation of good news as it was conceived of by the writer and his community. Mark begins with the baptism of Jesus by one who was certainly in many ways his rival and ends with three fear-struck women who told no one of the empty tomb "because they were afraid." Matthew, adding the Quelle sayings, begins with a genealogy tracing Jesus' lineage back to Abraham and his miraculous conception "by the Holy Spirit." He picks up some parables and miracle stories from Mark, adds other of his own material and ends not only with Jesus' resurrection but the great commission. Luke picks up much from Mark and Matthew, does some major redaction of Matthean texts, adds his original material (the prodigal son, the good samaritan and the road to Emmaus), rearranges the Quelle sayings and ends with the ascension of Jesus into heaven.

All but the Quelle sayings seem to have originated with the gospel writers or with members of their communities. Paul gives no evidence of having known of the birth narratives or the miracles. The Gospel of Thomas has only the sayings. A reasonable conclusion is that the Jesus of the gospels, apart from the earlier sayings, is a fiction. This is not to say that the gospel portrayals of Jesus suggest a different person than he was. The personality of Jesus that emerges, at least in the synoptic gospels, seems more or less consonant with the tenor of the sayings reasonably attributed to him. But it is to say the birth narratives, miracle stories and the passion narratives are not history but myth — smaller truths spun into a larger fiction with the intention of conveying what the spinners perceive as or wish were truth.

"Myth," of course, is a much misunderstood and misused word. It is not the opposite of truth. It is a vessel in which truth can be expressed sometimes better or more clearly than a prosaic, chronicling of events as they happen. Frank Frick, a scholar of the Hebrew scriptures, says, "Unfortunately in the popular mind the word 'myth' has come to mean a story with no foundation in fact, a sheer fiction, falsehood or fantasy. ... The Greek word *muthos* from which our word 'myth' stems originally meant simply 'something said' " (*A Journey Through the Hebrew Scriptures,* Frank S. Frick, 1995, Harcourt Brace and Co., p. 115). So the preacher, the Sunday School teacher and the catechist will need to begin in their preaching and teaching to distinguish between sayings and myth and stop treating Jesus as if he were a clearly knowable person from history rather than a figure about whom little is known for certain and who is portrayed as something he was not. But as a mythic figure, Jesus, called Christ or anointed one, can represent the human need and longing for a salvific figure. Thus, firmly based on those early sayings, preachers and teachers can credibly say that the ethical wisdom contained in and expressed by those sayings attained over time that larger-than-life status they still possess because second- and third-generation Christians, in an effort to build an entity that could compete successfully with other religions, placed the sayings in a mythic, cultic context complete with "stories" that gave their author a personality, history and divinity.

The one term remaining to be dealt with is the word "only," as in "only Son." It is no longer — if, indeed, it ever was — helpful to claim that Jesus of Nazareth was or is some exclusive revelation of god. In the first place, there are no objective and verifiable data to support such a proposition. It might be credible to propose for discussion that in the sayings attributed to Jesus there is to be perceived some uncommon goodness and wisdom that one would both wish and hope expresses the nature of a source/orderer. Into that discussion it would be necessary to admit other figures of history for consideration. It is reasonable to believe that a source/orderer may have disclosed itself at different times and places throughout human history. It is also reasonable to believe that one of those times and places was "under Pontius Pilate" in the person of Jesus and in the continuing community that formed around his teaching. It is finally reasonable to believe that similar disclosures have been made, are being made and will be made wherever and whenever.

It is thus ludicrous for 20th-century Christians to continue to make outlandish claims for Jesus. It is better to ponder if or how, in the slim body of ethical wisdom attributed to Jesus, a source/orderer might be attempting to engage whoever among human beings will be so engaged. Or, as it has been otherwise put, let those who have ears hear.

V

"He was conceived by the power of the Holy Spirit
and born of the Virgin Mary."

We are now deep into myth. The mythmakers were making a good faith attempt to tie the almost lost figure of Jesus to the unseen god in terms that would portray Jesus as the scion of that god and, therefore, as the fourth evangelist will put it, "the Word made flesh." This clause of the creed finds its biblical source in Matthew 1:18-25, Luke 1:26-2:20 and more obliquely in John 1:1-18. The argument seems to be that Jesus could not possibly be divine in origin if the divine had no special role to play in his conception. So the living presence (Holy Spirit) of god in some way fertilized Mary's ovum and, mirabile dictu, deus homo! The church would quarrel about the precise meaning of all this through the docetic and Arian controversies for more than 300 years. Jesus, by the way, was not the only deus homo to be proclaimed as such in the Greco-Roman world.

What are we to make of all this at the close of the 20th century? We can continue as some do to proclaim and perpetuate myth as objective truth, which would be irrational in the extreme. Or we can regard myth as myth and realize that it is the tissue of our longing to believe that the things Jesus may have said, viz; "Love your enemies ... as you want people to treat you, do the same to them ... ask and it will be given to you," represent in some way what may be at the heart of the universe's intelligence and will. That, then, can become the rational substance of the mythic language "was conceived by the power of the Holy Spirit and born of the Virgin Mary."

As to Mary, she makes appearances by that name in the birth narratives of Matthew and Luke. A mother of Jesus unnamed appears standing near the cross in John 19:25. Mark 6:3 (parallel in Matthew 13:55) mentions Mary as Jesus' mother and includes mention of brothers and sisters. Luke mentions Mary as Jesus' mother in Acts 1:14 and adds a note about some brothers. John never seemed interested in Jesus' mother except in the story of the miracle in Cana, where she is also unnamed, and the scene at the cross. Otherwise the maternal figure appears or is referenced in parallel narratives: Matthew 12:46 ff, Mark 3:31 ff. and Luke 8:19 ff. The Mary of the Matthean birth narrative is virtually absent, mentioned only in passing as being engaged to Joseph, discovered as pregnant "with child from the Holy Spirit" and at some juncture having given birth. By contrast, Luke's Mary is much more present and active. She is depicted as getting the word about her extraordinary state from an angelic messenger, whereas Matthew has the angel speak to Joseph.

Mary appears to have had several other children, according to the synoptics, presumably all younger — at least for Matthew and Luke, each of whom stresses the virginity aspect. Matthew can be given a pass on this issue since he used the Septuagint's translation of Isaiah 7:14, which renders the Hebrew "almah," young women, into the Greek "parthenos," which means virgin. "Almah" is the feminine of "elein," which means young man. "Almah" is translated in three other places in the Old Testament as "young woman." Luke, we assume, picked up Matthew's bare-bones birth narrative and turned it into a two-chapter blockbuster absent Matthew's "fulfillment" clause. The Hebrew scriptures apparently were of lesser importance to Luke than to Matthew who repeatedly uses the fulfillment formula, "All this took place to fulfill what had been spoken by the Lord through the prophet."

In any event the virgin birth of Jesus as an article of faith is based on the airiest of surmises, plus a bad translation of a key word. It is an unnecessary prop in the myth anyway. Besides, as New Testament scholar M. Eugene Boring points out: "The modern interpreter needs to know what Matthew and all his readers surely knew, that there were many stories of heroes and special personages who were 'sons' or 'daughters' of God through miraculous conception" (*The New Interpreter's Bible*, Vol. VIII, 1995. Abingdon Press, p. 137).

Jesus was probably born of some woman of the peasant class in Galilee sometime around the beginning of the first century C.E. or at the end of the prior century. He came to public attention, we might credibly guess, as one who rose up as a champion of the peasant class which sought to cope with the economic and social depredations of the Roman government of occupation. Which brings us to ...

VI

... "He suffered under Pontius Pilate, was crucified,
died and was buried..."

All of these past-tense verbs may represent the truth about

Jesus' demise, except perhaps the last. If he was put to death by crucifixion, his body may have been eaten by wild animals. The corpses
of crucified ones were often left exposed to the elements as the final
insult, making easy prey for wild animals and birds. That might explain the absence of a body which, in the gospels, is dealt with in the
resurrection and ascension narratives. In any event, Jesus surely at
some point died and maybe was buried. It is the cause and circumstances of his death that are of interest here and to what degree his
death had anything to do with the Judean procuratorship of Pontius
Pilate, 26-36 C.E. All four canonical gospels bring Jesus to Judea
and Jerusalem — the synoptics once and John thrice. But the Roman
occupation included Galilee, so where precisely and when a clash
may have come between Jesus and the authorities is not important.
And maybe such a clash never occurred.

Burton Mack likens Jesus to the wandering "cynics" of the
early first century C.E. — itinerant street speakers who traded in the
pithy, oblique critiques of manners and mores. They could be compared, if only for purposes of this discussion, with the curmudgeonly
newspaper columnist or the radio talk show host of today. Any one of
them would have been small potatoes to the Romans unless their public
utterances threatened to incite revolution. An examination of the Quelle
sayings or those in the Gospel of Thomas does not immediately suggest that a rabble-rousing agenda was being pursued — unless the
exaltation of the poor and the contention that the kingdom was among
them might have been considered subversive. If we had some clearer
idea of what it was Saul of Tarsus had been so eager to put down
before his conversion, we might understand what would possibly have
made Jesus obnoxious to the authorities.

In a "son of god" myth, Jesus could not be depicted as dying
by accident, illness or of old age — not if he is to be regarded as the
messiah and, more than that, the son of god, co-eternal, etc., etc. His

death must be noble; it must fulfill the relevant prophesies and have an encompassing effect. And it must come purposefully. Thus does Luke's narrative depict Jesus on a long pilgrimage from Galilee to Jerusalem. John puts Jesus on a straight path from the cleansing of the Temple in Chapter 2 to the cross in Chapter 19. Mark makes it clear that Jesus is working his way toward death straight from the first preaching in Capernaum, where people assert that a "new teaching" has been proclaimed, this time "with authority" and not like the scribes and the Pharisees. Thus was the fat in the fire. The narratives move along, a radical teaching here, a miracle there, an overturning of a social convention elsewhere. It is brought to a head in Jerusalem where the religious authorities find him a pretender and in no way fulfilling the messianic role. The Roman authorities are skittish about a populist uprising.

One can see Mark look up from his manuscript, scratch his head and wonder how credibly to take the story to the next step. Have the temple police arrest Jesus for the cleansing episode and let the law take its course? Have him assassinated? I think the evangelists made a stab at one denouement with "the crowds" ("the Jews" in John) depicted as loudly demanding crucifixion (Matthew 27:22-23, Mark 15:13-14, Luke 23:21-23 and John 19:6). But a populist lynching could not be a credible way for a messianic son of god to die. Enter Judas Iscariot, a character from central casting with a quintessentially Judean — as opposed to Galilean — name, a suspected pilferer (John 12:6). Judas is made by all four canonical evangelists to set the death machinery in motion. It remained for Luke and John to blame it on the Power of Evil: "Then Satan entered into Judas" (Luke 22:3) and "The devil had already put it into the heart of Judas, son of Simon Iscariot, to betray him" (John 13:2). So Jesus' death was not only to be a confrontation between Jewish and Roman authorities and Jesus but between the cosmic principalities and powers. It will also have a sacrificial aspect reminiscent of the suffering servant of Isaiah (53:4-6), especially "the Lord has laid on him the iniquity of us all." And who of all people but the high priest of the Temple, one Caiaphas, to suggest that "it was better to have one person die for the people."

So all the bases have been touched. Jesus is dead, to be sure. But as to how or by whose hand is unclear. But the story grew and grew into the myth it is today. And what truth of the matter is conveyed in that myth? Perhaps that the ethical wisdom of Jesus, countercultural as it is (Turn the other cheek. Love your enemies), has challenged and nettled so many for so long and has been more honored in the breach than the keeping, that what Jesus may have been and the teachings attributed to him have been put to death countless times over.

VII

"On the third day he rose from the dead..."

What else could be expected in light of the death of the "son of god?" We have already seen how the myth includes the sacrificial aspect, Jesus' dying in the place of others. So if god is just, Jesus must be restored to the life he didn't deserve to leave. In ways then, left unexplained, he descends to the place of the dead and comes back. "Lo, I am with you always even to the end of the ages."

How very much those who crowd into churches on Easter want to believe all that actually happened and that it means what Paul and others have said it means for human beings (see I Corinthians 15:15, 42-53). At the same time it is inescapably a fact that the Easter proclamation, which cannot be separated from the rest of the myth, is framed in a perspective foreign to the worldview on which our common life is based and, some would say, depends. Mary Wollstonecraft Shelley's fiction to the contrary notwithstanding, no observable data

24

have ever credibly been put forth to suggest that the reversal of death beyond a certain point, say three days, is possible or even desirable. Of course, we hear from time to time fantastic stories of near-death experiences, of the resuscitation of ones whom careless emergency or medical personnel have left for dead. Or we see on the way through the supermarket checkout line the screaming tabloid headlines about a corpse being prepared for embalming which proves, after all, to have a heartbeat. But that is not at all the kind of experience the gospels are talking about when they tell of Lazarus' return to life or of Jesus' under similar circumstances. The story of Lazarus is about the reanimation of dead tissue (that's the meaning of the three days in the tomb) resulting in the re-creation of a person in recognizable form. The difficulty Cleopas and his unnamed companion on the road to Emmaus (Luke 24: 13-35) and Mary Magdalene (John 20: 14-16) are depicted as having in recognizing the supposedly resurrected Jesus may suggest that Jesus' was not quite as bodily a resurrection as was Lazarus'. Whatever. It is the "recognizability factor" that is the important factor of these stories for people who do not wish to face the inevitable without some reassurance that their chemical and molecular structures will not simply become botanical nutrients.

So what do we say about the Easter proclamation that makes any sense in the world of thought framed by the Enlightenment and given substance by Copernicus, Galileo, Newton, Darwin, Freud and Einstein? I had to travel halfway around the world to a refugee camp to discover the 20th-century meaning of the Easter myth. I met a man there, a Vietnamese who had fled the Viet Cong's brutal repatriation of Saigon — now Ho Chi Minh City — but not before losing his business, his house and not before witnessing his wife and her family hacked to death with bayonets and their corpses shredded by machine gun fire. After about a year of unspeakable torture and imprisonment, he was released and subsequently joined several dozen other refugees at the edge of the sea where he and they became part of the now well-known "boat people." The boat on which he was a passenger was set upon by pirates who looted what few possessions the refugees had — all before capsizing the fragile craft. Eventually he and several others were rescued by the crew of a merchant freighter and ended up in a detention center in Hong Kong. In the 19 months of being interned there, he fell in love with a fellow refugee and they were married by a Vietnamese Catholic priest, though who knows if or how they ever enjoyed the intimacy proper to marriage.

In due course, the government of Hong Kong sent them and many others back to Vietnam. Not a week after their arrival, the newlyweds were separated; she was arrested, interrogated and summarily executed for some real or imagined crime. The man was sent to yet another camp — at Aranyaprathet, on the eastern border of Thailand where I found him in July 1979. After he had told me his story, I, struggling for the right words, fell back on my pastoral training and said something like, "Surely your religious faith (he was Catholic) helped you survive this incredible ordeal." Those, as it turns out, were the wrong words. His reply was polite but firm. He said that he had abandoned belief in God. The man was some kind of group leader among the refugees in his section of the camp. He was often smiling and seemed full of optimism about his and others' futures. One of the last things he said to me in our hour-long interview was, "They kill two wives of mine and they thought to kill me, too. But I am not dead, not yet." And he said it with a smile that seemed a mix of defiance and mirth. That's Easter without the myth. It is to say that despite the inevitability of death and the random suffering and loss that we will certainly encounter, there is meaning in and to life to be discovered in ourselves — who and what we are. The significance of the Easter myth may be that those who at first associated and identified with Jesus and his ethical and wisdom teachings discovered inexplicably that he lived on in them and their transmission and practice of those teachings.

It is therefore unfortunate that so many Christian clergy use the one Sunday of the year when their pews are actually full to rehearse the same delusional and intellectually bankrupt business about empty graves and the literal, physical resurrection of Jesus. Such clergy create great difficulties for people who are sincerely seeking some form of religious experience and connection without being forced to deny the fundamental principles of the Enlightenment. Clergy who do their homework know, of course, that the resurrection proclamation found in scripture is by no means unique in antiquity. They also know that it originated with the canonical gospels which came into the form in which we have them now at least 35 to 40 years after the events they depict. The resurrection narratives are, therefore, suspect as anything approaching factual accounts. It is known further that the gospels were never meant to be taken as factual accounts and were, instead, narratives spun to create an image of a godlike human being out of a Galilean peasant about whose life precious little is known. Christians attribute many sayings to him, credit him with extraordinary acts that defy natural law and end up portraying him as a god who dies in the place of sinful creatures to satisfy the bloodlust of an impossible god, and, on top of that, who comes back from the dead.

A far more plausible proposition is that those first century folk who rallied around the ethical and wisdom teachings found in their rally the strength and courage to endure and prevail in a terrible life under a repressive regime.

(Because belief in the resurrection has been so central a term of Christian faith, an appendix to this book may be found in which the New Testament texts having to do with the resurrection are closely examined as to what they say and do not say.)

VIII

*"He ascended into heaven and sits
on the right hand of the Father..."*

Once the mythic elements of the previous clauses have been acknowledged, it does not take much effort to construe the ascension. Once you have in whatever terms proclaimed a resurrection, eventually you'll be served with a habeas corpus petition. "If he's resurrected, we'd like to see him as you say you have," not unlike Thomas as depicted in John 20:24-25. You can stall only so long before it becomes necessary to honor the petition, if you could, or change your tune.

The ascension is implicit in Matthew 28:16-20, explicit in Luke 24:50-53 and unmentioned by Mark, John or Thomas. In John's account, the impression is given that Jesus in his risen form keeps hanging around (John 20:19ff, 26ff and 21:4ff). So only for Luke did it seem necessary to complete the mythic portrayal by having Jesus reunited with his father in the place of honor with the right to succession. Paul quotes some earlier formula in Philippians 2:5-11, which includes the words, "God also highly exalted him." And the writer of I Timothy includes another creedal statement that speaks of Jesus being "taken up in glory" (I Timothy 3:16). So the record is mixed. The myth demands an ascension. And it fits in with the worldview of the first century in which "heaven" or "the heavens" were believed to be the sacred realm of the gods. They were what you could see hints of by looking up. The planets and stars were the light of the glory of the gods seeping through the firmament. The Greek philosopher Plato whose ideas had infiltrated Hebraic thought long before the first century C.E. put plenty of stock in the invisible realm of the perfect forms. It was a place or a state in which a resurrected deus homo should dwell.

The observable "heavens" since Copernicus and Galileo and into the era of modern astrophysics have helped us to work out a quite different worldview than that of the first century. In our worldview there is no place for the heaven or heavens of the scriptures, no objectifiable category of meaning for them. So to say "he went to heaven" or "she will go to heaven when she dies" is, of course, nonsensical. To say that Jesus ascended into heaven and occupies the place of honor at god's right hand might be an elliptical way of saying that what his teachings represented and continue to represent is what we wish the world and all worlds to be like. It is to express the intention to live by those teachings and, by example, to convince other people to do, so that Jesus might indeed be exalted in the lives of those who follow him.

IX

"He will come again to judge the living and the dead ..."

This is an acknowledgment that Jesus' life and teachings, much less the miracles he is depicted as having brought about and the monumental events of his sacrificial death and resurrection, did not have the kind of effect necessary finally to bring in the rule (kingdom) of god. So he must "come again" to judge what he has not already redeemed. Of all the creed's clauses, this one has resulted in the most confusing welter of theological nonsense yet. You have your premillennialists, you have your postmillennialists and millions of bushwhacked believers in between who don't know the difference. What they do know individually is that they won't live forever, that they haven't always lived rightly and that a god who would cause 10 commandments to be carved in stone may judge them unfit for whatever reward may be laid up for the just.

I have been and continue to be amazed at the cheerful readiness with which many Christians embrace the concept of a fiery last judgment — though it is almost always other people they have in mind to be the judged. I refer this phenomenon to my friends in psychiatry to figure out. It is beyond the scope of this inquiry.

We can thank Matthew, chief among the gospel writers, for the proposition of a last or final judgment. His lengthy narrative in chapters 24 and 25, especially 25:31-46, strongly echoed in Luke 16:19-31, have Jesus himself presaging a judgment. The social justice appeal of the sheep-and-goats (Matthew) metaphor and of Dives' just deserts (Luke) does not make it any easier to rationalize these texts. As we know from experience, sometimes justice is so exquisitely deserving that we deem it "poetic." Sometimes the bad guys get what they have coming. Just as often, though, they "get away," as we say, "with murder." We know, further, that a deliberate lie is as likely as not to catch up with the liar. And Edgar Allan Poe's "The Tell-Tale Heart" speaks convincingly of the persistence of the fact of a matter. Consequences of action and inaction are also quite predictable and follow naturally from the act or the omission. I've known few lifelong nonsmokers who have died of lung cancer. I've known few health-food aficionados who have died of colon cancer. I've known few regular exercisers who have died prematurely of heart disease. And I have known people who did the opposite in each case, and I've presided at many of their funerals. Farmers in Brazil are burning off hundreds of thousands of acres of rain forest to make room for beef cattle to assuage the hamburger hunger of the world. The deleterious effects of their rape of the land are well known, and the consequences predictable. Unabated overuse of fossil fuels has predictable consequences as well.

This is to say that final judgment on how we act or do not act, on what choices we make or do not make, both individually and corporately, will issue in the consequences which may or may not be visited upon this or that individual or groups of individuals. The scriptural note that the rain falls on the just and the unjust pretty much sums it up.

Much of what Jesus may have had to say and much that is attributed to him accurately or inaccurately does not touch directly upon the vast array of choices and potential actions one might make or take. Jesus' admonition to treat others as one would wish to be treated, however, may cover a lot of ground. Couple that to Newton's Third Law of Motion, that every action has an equal and opposite reaction, and you have an Enlightenment version of judgment.

X
"I believe in the Holy Spirit..."

Which Holy Spirit is that? The spirit that the Priestly writers said brooded over the vasty deep "in the beginning"? The windblown, pyrotechnic phenomenon that Luke wrote of in Acts 2? Or the draught of breath Jesus blew upon his disciples, John says, in one of those post-resurrection experiences? (John 20:22). Probably a combination of them all. In some ways the concept of an unseen presence that is around, maybe acting by indirection in nature and history, is less corrosive of reasoned belief than much of what we have thus far discussed. The source/orderer metaphor of earlier chapters fits rather well here. And belief in a "holy spirit" is more credible if one posits its long-term existence — at least from the beginning of the formation of the universe, as the Priestly writers envisioned it (Genesis 1:1ff) and always after that. But the idea that the "holy spirit" arrived among the Jesus community for the first time as Luke has it do in Acts 2 is a contrivance. Check out John's language in Chapter 14, Verse 15: "If you love me, you will keep my commandments. And I will ask the Father, and he will give you another Advocate, to be with you forever. ... You know him, because he abides with you, and he will be in you." One wonders if the "spirit" of this passage is also the "spirit" of John 20:22. If so, it is clearly and intimately related to Jesus himself. The language of 14:17 ("You know him, because he abides with you...") must be a veiled reference to the early communities' living memory of Jesus, kept alive by the rehearsal and practice of his ethical and wisdom teaching. In that sense, the "spirit" of Jesus remained and, no doubt, strengthened those who followed in his way. The scene John envisioned (20:22) was probably an attempt to confer authority on the emerging third generation of church leaders by saying Jesus conferred authority on the first and they, by implication, on the second. This makes sense if it is agreed that the Gospel of John was written in 90-95 A.D. The earlier passage in which Jesus is depicted as being willing, contingent on the disciples' obedience, to petition his divine father to send a permanent advocate for the apostolic community occurs in the gospel before the passion-resurrection narratives. Is it possible that, for John, the permanent advocate is the strange mix of flesh and spirit that he depicts Jesus as having been? See John 20:19 and 26 in which the evangelist depicts a non-corporeal Jesus coming through a shut door or merely appearing without physically entering the room. On the first of those occasions — being the first post-resurrection experience John depicts — Jesus confers the spirit via his own breath, certainly to some degree reminiscent of "the wind of God" that "swept over the face of the waters" in the Priestly writers' creation imagery and of "the breath of life" by which the creature fashioned from the dust of the ground in the Jahwist's version.

Thus, perhaps the connection is made between the rest of the natural order and the first-century C.E. communities dedicated to Jesus, viz., that they spring from the same source/orderer. The prologue to John (1:1-18) is pretty clear in connecting the "word made flesh" to the logos without whom "not one thing came into being." Rather than being some separate person of what is called a triune god, what Christians call the holy spirit may be considered the non-material presence of a kinetic intelligence that may or may not have to do with the processes of nature and the ebb and flow of history.

"The holy catholic Church..." Here we leave the realm of the speculative and enter life and history as they actually can be known. And here is where the differences between the terms "believe" and "believe in" come into sharp relief. One cannot, despite his or her annoyance with the church or a wish that it had never been, say the church has not existed or does not exist. So with this clause of the creed, the issue is does one "believe in" the church? "Believe in" implies trust that the "believed-in" will perform as advertised, will do no harm to the believer and will be the believer's advocate. However, as with the promise of another advocate, the church's disposition toward those who believe in it is contingent upon their obeying the church's laws. Here, of course, things become instantly more complex. You have a church which claims it is *the* church, and its laws say divorced persons cannot take communion if they remarry without an ecclesiastical annulment of the prior marriage. You have this same church outlawing abortion, contraception and euthanasia. The prohibitions appeal to its divine authority to declare what is god's will. Other bodies which say they, too, are churches within the embrace of "the holy catholic Church" have their own idiosyncratic rules and prohibitions. One such church has recently dedicated itself to the conversion of American Jews.

Since the church in whatever shape and form it takes is first, last and in every instance a human institution, "believing in" it becomes problematic. In the first chapter, I wrote about believing in my wife of 17 years. That trust has been built on a day by day intimacy of shared respect, affection, responsibility and aspiration. I believe in her as I believe in no other. I cannot rationally extend that profound a trust to others whom I do not know, much less to a bureaucracy, of which I am just one constituent, that may not have my best interests at heart. Likewise, I cannot give unquestioning obedience to the laws and prohibitions of such an institution because I do not "believe in" it. I believe it exists, and I am a part of it. It does many good and decent things; it is generally benign and intends to be helpful. However, it has had its malign episodes. Its treatment of so-called heretics has been monstrous. The Crusades were tragic and mistaken fiascoes. The Episcopal Church in the mid-19th century did not distinguish itself on the issue of slavery. At least the Methodists and Baptists split into north and south over it. The almost universal homophobia of American Christianity is a scandal. The Presbyterians decide that celibate, nonpracticing homosexuals can be ordained. How generous! The Episcopal Church has recently concluded proceedings against one of its bishops who knowingly ordained a gay man who was in a monogamous and faithful relationship. The ecclesiastical court is to be congratulated for having dismissed the charges brought by other bishops, an action that ought never to have been taken. On the slimmest and most questionable scriptural analysis, many Christians — some of whom might be expected to know better — claim it is the divine will and church tradition that homosexuality and homosexual genital relations are forbidden. The utter illogic of that position seems to escape its proponents. If their god is the maker of all that is seen and unseen, then it is the maker of the homosexual disposition, and if their god looked out at its creation and said, "Behold, it is very good," how is homosexuality and the sexual behavior that proceeds from it evil?

The church has often enough been and sometimes still is today a repressive institution. Beyond the level of the local faith community, it is an abstraction — and sometimes a dangerous one. Better people should, where trust has been built, believe in one another as communities are built person by person. Believing in abstract and remote structures is not rational.

"The communion of saints..." If it is possible to construe this term of antiquity to mean something like "I believe in who we are, what we're doing and how we're doing it," a credible humanism would be the result. "The communion of saints" appears in the baptismal creed as an extension of the Holy Spirit. Historians say it was added to the creed in the late fourth century and appears to have been added to give a clearer explanation of the nature of the church. Its meaning, though, is problematic. One way of interpreting it is the way Protestants have interpreted it since the Confession of Augsburg in 1530, in which the church was the *congregatio sanctorum,* or gathering of the saints or the assembly of all believers. An earlier, if not the original, intent of the clause is that the church militant has a connection or "communion" with the church triumphant and particularly with the holy martyrs of antiquity, whose blood was the seed of the continuing and growing church. But there is no reason to view the two interpretations as mutually exclusive. I feel that a connection exists between the first-century peasant follower of Jesus and me as I write op-ed columns and preach sermons advocating economic and social justice based on those early sayings attributed to Jesus. Though the price of my advocacy for the economic counterculture has not been dramatically costly, I can identify with those for whom it has been. A "communion of saints" surely exists among the living and the dead, embracing such figures as Mohandas Gandhi, Cesar Chavez, Martin Luther King, Abraham Lincoln and others the reader might name.

Yet what contemporary Christians need to do is to seek communion/connection not based on shared ideology but on shared purpose and intention. As ones who take to heart the admonition to treat others as they wish to be treated and intend to make that principle operative by turning the other cheek, walking the second mile, giving the coat as well as the shirt and forgiving 70 times seven, contemporary Christians can reach across ideological, cultural, racial and sectarian boundaries to help form a human communion that may exalt the human agenda of economic justice, intellectual freedom and social mobility. The belief that lies at the base of this "communion" is that the human being is a creature of enormous potential, of great emotional depth and intellectual possibility. This creature must be given every opportunity to be liberated from crippling and repressive economic, social, educational and religious institutions and ideas so that each person may attain that of which he or she is capable.

The human genome is a telling feature of the "communion" that obtains amongst homo sapiens. So is the apparent but astonishing proposition that any individual is only six degrees separated from knowing every other human being, so vast and complex is the internet of people. Person A will know to some extent 200 other people, each of whom will know 200 others, some of whom may be people that Person A also knows or has known. And so it goes. In the end, all human beings are related. Plasma is interchangeable according to compatible type. Life, liberty and the pursuit of happiness are universal values. So to profess belief in a "communion of saints" in late 20th-century terms is to announce an intention to work for peace, racial and social harmony, economic justice and equity, the preservation of the environment, poverty, homelessness, full educational opportunities, reproductive rights, the right to end one's own life in extremis — and to do so regardless of provincial, national, racial, political or sectarian identity. Such a program might well include aggressive efforts to bring down such tyrants as Hussein of Iraq and Assad of Syria and the mad psychiatrist and his general friend who have made Bosnia one massive killing field. One need not be an absolute pacifist to affirm belief in a pan-global unity of human beings.

"The forgiveness of sins..." We approach now the goal toward which the previous clauses of the creed have been heading: sal-

vation. All the monumentally significant concepts and events it posits up to now lead to a ticket to "the resurrection of the body and the
life everlasting" before which the forgiveness of sins must be effected.
The word to watch out for here is "sins." "Sin," says Wolfhart
Pannenberg, "means going astray, failing to find the source of life in
our search for life" (*The Apostles' Creed In Light of Today's Questions*, 1972, The Westminster Press, p. 164). "Sins" is not the title of
a laundry list of major and minor wrongs. It attempts to describe a
rather normal state of being, vis-a-vis a perceived source/orderer, being out of harmony with, if not arrayed against, the more or less obvious flow of things. Water seeks its level. The apple loosed from its
branch will fall to the ground. Beached fish die. Overeating makes
one fat. Drinking too much makes one drunk. Spending more than
one earns invites bankruptcy. Each of these examples is either "how
things are" or "what happens when." Water by itself will not run up-
hill any more than an apple will fall upward. Overconsumption has
its predictable outcome. That suggests that there is a natural flow of
things, certain "givens" that one opposes to his or her own discom-
fort, displeasure or destruction.

The Mosaic code, often called the Ten Commandments, must
have arisen at a time in Israel's history when it was struggling to
figure out what in human relationships worked and what didn't. Giving the community's highest loyalty to an unseen god was insurance
against a member of the community's attempt to make himself or
herself god and so subjugate other members. Covenanting to have
but one god made for communal solidarity. Further covenanting to
honor elders helped build a jurisprudential and cultural history and
tradition. Prohibiting murder, adultery, theft, false witness and envy
created — or represented the intention to create — a secure and dependable society. For that ancient community, the source of life was
its covenant, its Torah, and to seek "life" apart from its "source" (to

apply Pannenberg's analysis) was to "sin."

Among late 20th-century persons drawn to Christianity, it will be important to conceive of sin not so much as the sum total of individual crimes and misdemeanors but as societal trends and systems manipulated by individuals against individuals and groups against groups that marginalize others for the benefit or perverse pleasure of the marginalizers. It will be likewise important to understand that pervasive and undue interference with the environment in ways that defy clear natural purpose and process is to seek life apart from seeking communion with its source. It is finally important for any person to acknowledge that he or she has been less than human far too often and that injuries and offenses given in moments of time now past and irretrievable cannot be taken back. And in so far as individually given injuries and offenses may participate in systemic human diminishment, the lesson needs to be learned, internalized and acted upon henceforth. Was it this understanding of the past as prologue that at least in part motivated the recent public confessions of former segregationist George Wallace, who rued his racist past, or of former Secretary of Defense Robert McNamara as tearfully he told of having been mistaken 50,000 lives ago? Does then forgiveness of sin, as we might say, come in being openly and honestly self-shriven and going on from there changed and chastened? And what part in any or all of that is required of the community? Is Wallace forgiven if the relatives of Medgar Evers are unreconciled? Is McNamara shriven if the widows and orphans of the Vietnamese war dead remain unconsoled?

The point of forgiveness is closure and justice. One of the most admirable human qualities is contrition — to discover and to acknowledge wrongdoing and to seek to make amends. Contrition is useful precisely because it helps effect closure and a sense that something that needs to be over is over.

"The resurrection of the body and the life everlasting..." At

this point in the recitation of the creed, many Christians make upon themselves the sign of the cross. What that surely signifies at some level is that this concluding cause is the most important of all and has been the point all along. The need to believe in immortality must be very old among homo sapiens. I acknowledge that need in my own self even as I acknowledge the irrationality of the whole idea. If there were something beyond death of a positive nature in human beings' future, why is the instinct of self-preservation so intense in us? Perhaps that instinct suggests that at some level we know that life is limited in length so that the psalmist had it about right when he or she wrote: "So teach us to number our days," or the second Isaiah when he wrote, "The grass withers; the flower fades. Surely the people is grass." Limited, I say, in length. But length is not the only dimension. Breadth and depth are others of greater importance because individuals, with enough freedom and opportunity, can make their lives as broad and as deep as they make the effort to do so. Wolfgang Mozart lived only into his mid-30s, but what breadth and depth that life made! Part of the reason people approach Jack Kevorkian for his help in ending their lives is that, due to circumstances of health, the length of life is threatening the value of its breadth and depth.

In one sense, the hope of immortality, or as the creed states it, "resurrection and life everlasting," is very endearing. We like ourselves, and we like those we have come to love. We do not wish to contemplate a time when we and they are no more. So we have constructed over time two complicated ideas of what happens after death — and the two are not compatible. The one is that upon death the "soul," a non-corporeal entity that might be compared to Freud's "ego," departs from the body and goes off to "heaven." The remains, as they are called, are exactly that. Except people in funeral homes comment upon how "natural he looks" and later at the cemetery are content to erect gravestones that bear the legend "Here lies..." The second idea, which is more in line with biblical terms, is that the person who dies is dead — body, mind, spirit, whatever. The dead person is buried or cremated, and the survivors rehearse the hope of an eventual resurrection (see I Corinthians 15:35-52). That would presumably entail a reconstitution of the body's chemical or molecular structure.

Either idea is appealing, but neither is rational nor is either based upon a single empirical datum. And both, if we admit it, are products of highly creative and imaginative wishful thinking. If we return to the concept of a source/orderer, it might be possible to rationalize this terminal clause of the creed as actually meaning that those who die are returned in one way or another to the cosmos out of which, atom by atom, they came through the processes of evolution, conception, gestation and birth. Beyond that, anything is speculation, need-based hope or irrational and delusional propaganda.

This first section has been an argument for a rational analysis of an ancient creed and a proposal to move beyond it. The creeds we will always have with us, even as we have the books of Leviticus and Numbers — important documents of our religious tradition but virtually useless today. The Episcopal Book of Common Prayer includes in its pages (864-878) what it calls "Historical Documents of the Church." They include the conclusion of the Council of Chalcedon (451 C.E.), the Creed of St. Athanasius and the Articles of Religion dated 1571. Perhaps the proper place for the Apostles' and Nicene Creeds is in this section of the Prayer Book where they can be seen for what they are: priceless documents of other times and worldviews which certainly help inform the worldview that is evolving even now among Christians trying to be faithful.

Part Two:
Practical Implications

As the Christian community approaches the dawn of the 21st century, at least one aspect of its multifaceted life is clear: The traditionally conservative, evangelical Protestant churches are flourishing while the once-dominant mainline denominations — largely liberal in orientation — are in eclipse. Church growth gurus will insist that it is the liberal bias — if such exists — of those latter communities which is dooming them to irrelevance. I have made an oblique challenge of that opinion in Part I of this book wherein I attempted to articulate fundamental Christian beliefs in Enlightenment concepts and language appropriate to the times in which we find ourselves. The underlying premise of Part I is that for institutional Christianity to prevail as well as endure as a viable intellectual option, it will need to cease using the second- and fourth-century language of its major creeds and figure out what it can mean in the closing years of the 20th century to say, for example, "I believe in the resurrection of Jesus."

The same principle applies to one of the church's major activities: what it calls worship. I find myself much of the time mentally rolling my eyes at what I must say or hear as a leader of liturgy. It is not that I am an unbeliever; it is that I want and need to express my beliefs in concept and language that insofar as possible is congruent with the understandings through which human beings have come to appreciate how things are and work in as much of the universe that has been probed by various kinds of scientific disciplines. So, too, the content of worship or liturgy must for me and, I am persuaded, for many, many Christians, be rethought, restructured and restated.

For better or worse, the Episcopal Church has been my home in one way or another for going on 40 years. Hence the Book of Common Prayer has been my guide to liturgy and theology — lex orandi, lex credendi. Like so many Episcopalians, I was early on aesthetically enamored of the Prayer Book's language, so stately and cadenced was it. I say "was" because the Standard Book of Common Prayer (1979) is a different creature in many important ways from its predecessor (1928). But here's the thing: The 1979 Prayer Book, while improved theologically in so many ways, does not go nearly far enough. The Prayer Book did not need to be revised, as it turns out, but virtually razed, rethought and built again from the ground up.

For one thing, the 1979 Prayer Book shows little attention to gender-neutral language, and it was being brought to completion in the first years in which women priests were being lawfully ordained! But that's not the worst of it. The revised baptismal liturgy still has sponsors renouncing "Satan and all the spiritual forces which rebel against God." Rather than fret and complain about the inadequacy and irrelevance that too often makes liturgy frustrating to the intellect, I will herein attempt to set forth theological underpinnings for several experimental liturgical forms that may be used with intellectual honesty in the coming millennium.

I am not free to use them in any regular public manner in the congregation I serve and I would not put my bishop in the position of having to discipline me for their uncanonical use. Neither would I subject a congregation, most members of which do not at this time find themselves in the place I am, to the use of such experimental forms. What I am doing is laying before whatever interested parties there may be a few ideas for serious discussion with an eye to a future more might share.

THE EUCHARIST

The presence in the 1979 Book of Common Prayer of two distinct rites for the celebration of the eucharist is the most obvious clue to one of the primary dynamics present in the years-long revision process that began shortly after World War II and continued over the next 30 or so years. That dynamic was a political one: traditionalists against innovators with compromise, not always cheerfully arrived at, being the order of the day. Thus the 1979 Prayer Book is a patchwork of tradition and innovation that, to the uninitiated, must appear odd at best and goofy at worst. Why do what is called "Rite One" and what is called "Rite Two" coexist in the same book? Because the church elite that directed the revision could not and would not agree on a single rite. Some point to the two rites as a classic example of the Anglican nicety of the via media in which, under the flawed assumption that given sufficient concessions most will be pleased, hardly anyone is.

I find Rite One with its pseudo-Elizabethan cadences and terminology and, as well, its discredited theology to be a patent offense. Start with, "We have erred and strayed from thy ways like lost sheep" (from the General Confession, BCP 1979, page 320). Lost sheep are lost because sheep are generally stupid, low-grade intelligence animals. Any human being whose intelligence matches that of a sheep will not know enough to confess his "manifold sins and wickedness" or "the devices and desires of [his] own heart." Who with any intellectual honesty can say that prayer and mean it? Archbishop Thomas Cranmer and his lot wrote most eloquently in the 16th century and perhaps the intelligentsia of that age could pray or say what they wrote. Some four hundred years later in a different world those expressions simply do not work.

So it is that Rite One of the Episcopal Prayer Book is a period piece absolutely worthy of preservation for some of the same reasons that William Shakespeare's plays are worth preserving. The former should be studied, analyzed and even enjoyed as aesthetically pleasing, but in no way should they be inflicted upon contemporary communities whose members are earnestly trying to cope with life at the end of the 20th century on its terms and in language and concept that make sense now.

That brings us to Rite Two (1979 Book of Common Prayer, pages 351-366) which, to be sure, includes many innovative aspects both as to intention and language, but ultimately fails to transcend the impossibly cramped and philosophically passe theology of other times not our own. It still, of course, includes that fourth-century document known as the Nicene Creed that was also a product of compromise. As was discussed in Part One, the Nicene confession is crafted in fourth-century terms based on fourth-century understandings that no longer work.

The canons (or prayers of consecration) of Rite Two still refer to "sacrifice" and to the bread and wine as being somehow the Body and Blood of Jesus which, of course, they are not in any possible sense of the word. One must wonder at the persistence of the idea that the death of Jesus of Nazareth exculpates those who believe he is "the Son of God" from the consequences of their "sins." Prayer A of Rite Two (pages 361-363) repeats the formula, "On the night he was handed over to suffering and death, our Lord Jesus Christ took bread; and when he had given thanks to you, he broke it, and gave it to his disciples, and said, 'Take, eat: this is my Body, which is given for you'... he took the cup of wine ... and said, 'Drink this, all of you: This is my Blood of the new Covenant, which is shed for you and for many for the forgiveness of sins...' " These formulae have clear connections to the cultic blood sacrifices of Israel's antiquity which even contemporary Judaism understands as part of its past but neither its present nor future.

Out of much pastoral experience and teaching in congregations, I can be safe in saying that many, if not most, people who receive communion do not believe they are receiving — even metaphorically — flesh and blood. They also do not believe that that particular bread and wine have any salvific effect for them, that Jesus, in other words, died for their sins.

So what is it people *do* believe about the eucharistic liturgy? Of what efficacy is it? What does it accomplish and how? From observable data, one can say the eucharistic liturgy brings people together in some kind of intentional community, and that, in a broken world, is no mean accomplishment. What a given community's intention may actually be on a given occasion would be hard to say. But that receiving communion seems to be the point, or at least a point, of the gathering is a clue to the largely unarticulated significance of that action. It is participatory; it is inclusive; it is egalitarian; it is, in fact, a common meal. Participation is, if you don't consider the stern requirements of some communities (days of obligation, for example), entirely voluntary. Inclusiveness is, if there is no local or jurisdictional rubric of closed communion, a welcome dynamic in a world of gated communities, glass ceilings, private clubs and economic and social barriers. The egalitarian nature of communion is evident in the common portion of bread and the common cup.

Voluntary participation in an atmosphere of nondiscriminatory inclusion following egalitarian principles is a great part of the content of Jesus' wisdom as found here and there in the gospels, both canonical and otherwise. Participation, inclusion and egalitarianism are the dynamics of true democracy shared by true democrats but not often by the elite. I submit, therefore, that what most American Christians (in the case of this study, Episcopalians) are doing when they assemble for worship is cultivating and celebrating their freedom to fully participate, their automatic inclusion and the egalitarian nature of the gathering — all of which is affirming and supportive. What would be the nature of a eucharistic rite that would emphasize those elements and remain as true as possible to biblical tradition?

The eucharistic liturgy needs to be grounded far more thoroughly than at present in the words Jesus is most likely to have said — that is, if it is agreed that he valued inclusion and egalitarianism and free participation. In such a case, much of the mythological elements present even in the more contemporary eucharistic rites will have to be forgone in the knowledge that their inclusion in what was in antiquity probably a simple agape meal came about through primitive Christianity's immersion in Greek mythological thought forms and language in the first two or three centuries of the Common Era. Such mythology was replete with dying sons of the gods, resurrections, ascensions and the like, not to forget miraculous births. To paraphrase New Testament scholar Robert W. Funk, we need to free the Jesus of our common rites from all that if we wish to say what we mean and mean what we say.

Here follows, then, an outline for a eucharistic liturgy that will be accessible and credible for persons wishing to be religious and at the same time intellectually honest at the inception of the 21st century.

A local community identified as "Christian" will center itself on the teachings of Jesus by knowing what passages of the New Testament can reasonably be said to have come from him. The community will acknowledge the radical egalitarian nature of such teachings, their common wisdom and irenic tone. The community will examine its collective life and encourage individuals within it to do the same. All of this is to be an ongoing process of education, introspection and, where desirable, public testimony. How that might work in a given liturgy will become evident further on.

It is, say, a Sunday morning, and 150 or 200 members of Church of the Apostles are gathering for their weekly assembly. Several urns of coffee, juice and healthful munchies await the people in a comfortable and inviting common room. Children and youths eventually find their ways to classrooms, older youths and adults head for classes in bible, history, ethics — or perhaps stay together for a special speaker or forum on a topic pertinent to the local congregation.

At the end of the hour, all would return to the common room where announcements could be made, concerns lifted up, plans made and a general greeting similar to the pax shared.

A liturgical president, not necessarily an ordained person, might then begin the more formal aspect of the gathering by calling for a Quaker-type silence during which members would be invited to bid the attention of the community to recent incidents within and without the liturgical community that illustrate Jesus' teachings in action or that call for the intervention of the community by way of prophetic action, hands-on ministry or other service. This may be followed by other statements that account for failings of the community or its members in such ministries or service, with the resolve expressed to learn from mistakes of mission or commission. Members may also wish to ask for support for personal issues, crises or needs, with others assuring such members of the community's willingness and readiness to help.

Following that, one appointed to apply the learnings from the earlier educational hour may address the community, gathering up its concerns, needs, opportunities, problems and failures expressed or revealed that day, and, through exposition or analysis of biblical or other of the community's literature, help focus members' attention on a theme common to its life. Opportunity for dialogue, questions, commentary and response would be built in.

Then that day's president would call for the elements of a common meal to be brought to a focal point, say a central table. The president would then recall the community's heritage and history, perhaps using biblical quotations and other commonly known material, observing that the community's life is centered on the principles of voluntary participation, inclusiveness and egalitarianism, never forgetting the needs of the world outside the community and resolving to use the corporate strength of the members to meet those needs.

The president would then invite members to come by the table to partake of the elements of the meal as a sign of their unity and solidarity. Instrumental and/or vocal music might be offered during this time and joined in on where appropriate by members of the community.

Finally, the president would dismiss the community, reiterating its purpose, its mission and its weekly intention to gather. Members bid one another farewell until they meet again.

It will be noticed that no prescribed texts or definite rubrics have been proposed for the liturgy suggested above. Each local community should assemble, edit and adapt its own texts and attempt to ground them in the common Jewish-Christian literature. But the one-size-fits-all approach to liturgy, while it may appeal to the desire some may have to denominational or jurisdictional uniformity, tends to make local congregations into branch offices of some larger and abstract entity. The strength and effectiveness of the liturgy is in its local integrity as a true "work of the people," which is what "liturgy" means.

Surely, though, the various resources for liturgical texts, e.g., the Book of Common Prayer, can be claimed by local congregations to plan and execute liturgy, but because a local entity finds it important and desirable to do so, not because a central authority mandates it.

BAPTISM

Every community I know of has some form of an initiation or welcome rite, be it the Welcome Wagon, freshman hazing, swearing-in, orientation or — in the case of the church — baptism and confirmation. The question for the church is what its initiation rites should look like and be in the 21st century.

The revisions that Vatican II brought to the Roman Catholic rite of baptism, the spirit of which the Episcopal Church captured in part in the 1979 revision of its own initiation rite, give a sense that baptism is primarily a ritual of welcome and ingrafting of one into a visible community. The 1928 Episcopal rite laid heavy emphasis on regeneration and forgiveness. What is needed now is a complete re-thinking of the initiation rite so its words and actions mean what they say and show.

What is really happening when, say, a couple brings an infant to the church for baptism? On the basis of 30 years of pastoral experience with that phenomenon, I can say with some certainty that couples do not believe that their much adored babies need any forgiveness or regeneration. There does remain the superstitious notion that one unbaptized will not in some sense be "saved" or "go to heaven," but that is often the tactic used by well-intentioned grandparents to co-erce their children to bring grandchildren to the font. Actually, the question really is social acceptability. And so it is, too, for the parents. If you're going to be involved in a congregation at any significant level, you'll need to conform to its norms. Thus baptism as it is now widely practiced.

No doubt there should be some kind of welcome rite for a new baby just as there ought to be one for a new member or family in a congregation, because in either case there have come a brand new face or faces with names attached to them, and new members change a family or community. Thus it is appropriate to mark their arrival in some distinctive way.

Joining any community involves what I will term commitment and covenant. A joiner covenants with the already present community to take on its commitments and the mission that is in progress. In the case of a Christian congregation, the commitment is in one way or another to the ethical system based on Jesus' wisdom teachings. But more particularly the initiant (or, in the case of an infant or child of tender years, his/her sponsors) will covenant to join in the particular ministries of the congregation that flow from the general commitment to the Jesus teachings. In that respect, the last two vows of the 1979 Prayer Book's Baptismal Covenant are most appropriate: "Will you seek and serve (Jesus) in all persons, loving your neighbor as yourself?" and "Will you strive for justice and peace among all people, and respect the dignity of every human being?" (page 305).

The obvious humanism of these baptismal questions goes to the heart of the gospel. It is not subscription to theological abstractions that counts but a commitment to make a positive difference in and through one's life that 21st-century religion must be about. How then to rescue what is now called "baptism" from concepts and language that are alien to our time?

The first task is to inquire as to how we may understand the ideas of "salvation" and the "forgiveness of sins" in a 21st-century way. The word "sin" has a very complex philology. What it has come to mean in casual contemporary converse is something like a "really bad thing that isn't actually against the law but for which I feel pretty cruddy about having done." How one obtains "salvation" from the residual effects of such a thing in all probability has to do with making amends and learning from the mistake. That kind of penitential dynamic, given human nature, can and should be a continuing part of one's life. And initiation into an intentional Christian community might sometimes be an appropriate occasion for some humanistic act of contrition. One thinks again of the recantations and apologies of Robert McNamara and George Wallace for their lapses of courage and compassion, respectively, where the Vietnam War and militant segregation were concerned.

While public contrition may be appropriate to a community's initiation rite, it should not be mandatory. What needs to be mandatory is a kind of signing on to the ownership of the community's mission statement and more or less formal enrollment into one or another aspects of its mission and ministry. Each congregation ought to be able to craft language and liturgical action that will work for its life. Again, traditional rites are always resources to be used and adapted.

But what is a community to do about what is now known as "infant baptism" or "dedication" or "baby naming?" Desire for such a rite will not abate anytime soon, and there is an obvious need for something like it in any event. Conceiving and bearing of children into the world is about as profound a process as one can imagine. It partakes in the mystery of creation and thus is deserving of distinctive notice. Because a congregation is likely to affect the formation of one born into its life, the emphasis — or one emphasis — in any infant initiation rite might be on the congregation and its collective responsibility to the infant's parents and to the infant himself/herself over time.

The baptismal liturgy of the 1979 Prayer Book sums that up quite well in this question from officiant to gathered congregation: "Will you who witness these vows do all in your power to support this person in his/her life in Christ?" What the keeping of such a promise will look like will again depend on the nature of life in a given community, but it certainly should envision mentors and a small support group for each family presenting children — mentors and a support group that will stick with the formation task in the long term. Certainly more than one formal question and rote answer would be desirable — even the writing and formal signing of a covenant agreement for mentors, the support group and parents.

CONFIRMATION

What rite of passage in 20th-century American culture has been more celebrated than a) the pubescent ritual of the first driver's license or b) high school graduation? It is to those events that the church of the 21st century will want to key what is now confirmation because they have to do with the beginning of accepting adult responsibilities, though surely this rite of passage must also in certain important respects resemble the Jewish bar/bat mitzvah, which involves considerable study of religious history and literature. It might well include, beyond that, a kind of Peace Corps or Vista experience that points to the obligations inherent in being part of a community whose life focuses on the ethical program grounded in the wisdom teachings of Jesus.

In the Catholic traditions, which include among others the Episcopal Church, confirmation is often within the purview of the episcopal office, meaning that a figurehead of authority arrives deus-ex-machina out of the ecclesiastical ether and lays hands on persons largely unknown to him or her, signs certificates and goes on to the next congregation. The hierarchical nature of that process is bothersome. The agency of what we call confirmation needs to be the mentors and support groups with whom a youth has been involved from as close to the beginning as possible. They are the ones who should present to the gathered community youths to whose readiness for adult responsibility they can honestly attest. That is confirmation.

Congregations would do better to abandon the terms "baptism" and "confirmation" and call the 16- to 18-year process "formation," with initiation and adult passage rites at either end. Certainly the water and chrism rituals can be retained as long as their symbolism is explained in 21st-century terms. The application of water would signify the beginning of a life (or, in the case of a youth or adult, the beginning of a new phase of a life) — water being understood as the fundamental substance on which biological life depends. The chrism would signify the maturity of one who began the formation at the font. A 21st-century chrism might actually be common motor oil, thus connecting the rite to the driver's license and also to the fact that petroleum is the result of a long process of death and life, being that oil is a fossil fuel. [No doubt some have at this point put down this book and enjoyed a good laugh at the expense of the author. What? So olive oil makes more sense?]

One final note on confirmation: At least in the Episcopal Church's rite a candidate for confirmation is required to reaffirm his/her "renunciation of evil," to "renew your commitment to Jesus Christ" and to "follow him as ... Savior and Lord." That is all well and good as long as "evil" is understood to be those systemic and symptomatic things that rob persons of their dignity, liberty and life; as long as the "commitment to Jesus Christ" is understood as embracing the wisdom and gentleness found in his wisdom teaching, which will confer dignity, afford liberty and support life.

In the end, neither bishop nor priest/minister is needed to effect "confirmation" unless by chance he/she has been a significant part of the mentoring and/or support group process. The clergy's part in all of this is the core curriculum of religious studies — not as the conferring agency of an end-of-process honor. The rite of passage to adulthood must in no way be understood as a final terminus. The responsibilities to covenant, commitment, continued learning, service, ministry and stewardship only intensify with the onset of adulthood. For-

53

mation ideally goes on until death.

MARRIAGE

If any rite of the church needs major renovation, it is marriage — all the way from the ritual texts of most denominations to the strange and outrageous customs that have evolved into so-called "church weddings." I would consider it a major lifetime achievement if I could somehow end the use of churches as wedding chapels for the vulgar display of costly flowers, outlandish costumes and execrable music. It is flat-out immoral for the church to be party to such circuses that as often as not end up entailing the expense of $25,000 to $50,000.

In a country which so prizes separation of church and state, I cannot understand why clergy suffer themselves to be unpaid surrogate magistrates of the states, which they become once a marriage license comes into their possession. If a state wants to regulate marriage — and for all kinds of reasons it should — let the state execute marriage licenses and let religious communities bless, celebrate or recognize a state of being that obtains between two persons. Such blessings might best take place during regular gatherings of the community. It would be understood that persons would be considered fully and validly married if, for their own reasons, they did not wish to seek their community's blessing, or recognition. It is enough to celebrate others' happiness.

Costly gowns, veils and floral arrangements, none of which are ever used again and become, at best, mementos, and, at worst, attic or cellar space-takers, need to be excluded from churches along with unity candles, pew bows, candelabra, Wagner and Mendelssohn. All of that is, in any event, mostly the doing of the wedding industry encouraged by such movies as "Father of the Bride." Many an American girl has grown up believing that her life will be at its acme in that one bright and shining moment when, weighed down by pounds of satin and tulle, a $200 hairdo and a cosmetic job worthy of Holly-wood, she emerges at the end of the aisle on the arm of her proud papa into the full glare of the spotlight. Everything after that is down-hill.

The church has the moral obligation to rid itself of such produc-tions and to build into formation programs education and training that will provide youths and adults with acceptable alternatives to wedding extravaganzas. In no event should a congregation permit the latter. Until people can be educated as to what the church means or ought to mean when it undertakes to recognize and celebrate mar-riage, congregations might best refer their members to hotels, halls or other venues for weddings and offer to bless, recognize or cel-ebrate marriages during regular liturgies. This will not for some time be appreciated as the right way to go, but it is, and in time it will be seen as having been so.

As to the texts for marriage blessings, celebrations or recogni-tions, those in existence currently make little sense today. We can start with what some denominations, notably the Episcopal Church, include in the opening statement of the wedding service: "Marriage was established by God in creation, and our Lord Jesus Christ adorned this manner of life by his presence and first miracle at a wedding in Cana of Galilee. It signifies to us the mystery of the union between Christ and his Church..." (1979 Prayer Book, page 423).

How credible is it at the end of the 20th century to declare that God established marriage in creation? This statement is either an out-right a priori assertion or a reference to the Adam and Eve mythology of Genesis. Either way, it is unsupportable. What is true is that many, but by no means all, persons are sexually attracted to members of the opposite sex. Anthropologists will explain that such attraction has basically to do with the biological necessity and urge to reproduce. Monogamous marriage has turned out to be a most desirable manner in which to reproduce and care for the young. Marriage is also an economic arrangement, though that aspect of the estate was more obvious in other eras when agriculture was primarily a family venture. Husbands were needed to cultivate, plant and harvest land. Wives were needed to manage the household. Children were needed to help bear both sets of burdens.

Marriage is a thing also of companionship. The solitary life appears to appeal to a relatively few. Compatibility of couples who wish to make marital common cause is a special gift life sometimes affords. The profound bonding that comes of a pleasurable and happy sex life is certainly a primary benefit of marriage, and modern contraceptive procedures have helped humans to cultivate their sexual relationships without regard to reproduction. I call that real progress.

The preface to marriage in the Episcopal Prayer Book (page 423) cited earlier speaks of the purposes of marriage that were "instituted by God." We should rather observe that marriage has evolved over the human epoch into what at this juncture it is or, under realistic circumstances, can be. To whatever extent a source/orderer of the universe may have intended for marriage, or to whatever extent its experiment with humankind has produced marriage as we know it in its various cultural forms, is not knowable. This should be somehow acknowledged in a congregation's formation program and in blessings, recognitions or celebrations of marriages.

The "giving" of a daughter or even a son in marriage is a distasteful carryover from another time when especially female children were patriarchal possessions to give or to sell. Such ceremonial should be completely excised from congregational recognitions. In normal situations, a man and a woman have discovered and been attracted by and to one another. They, in effect, have given themselves to each other. That is what is to be recognized. The "giving in marriage" is heavily suggestive of arranged marriages that, at least for mainstream

56

contemporary American culture, are abhorrent.

There is also trouble with the vows couples exchange. For one thing, the common understanding of the vows is that their exchange marks the beginning of marriage — or that the officiant's pronouncement of marriage which follows upon the vows "marries" a couple. How often and painstakingly have I had gently to disabuse a couple of that notion. I explain that, by the time they have presented themselves to the congregation, a state of marriage must for all practical purposes exist, or the congregation has nothing to recognize or celebrate, unless it be a stated intention to begin a process that would eventually lead to the existence of the marital estate.

In this regard, congregations might well be advised to institute a kind of betrothal rite during which, at a regular gathering of the community, couples can announce such intentions and ask for the community's support and understanding as they move toward their realization. What an opportunity then is presented to a congregation to craft and institute in its formation program a continuing marriage preparation and maintenance program.

Second, there is trouble with the vow "until death us do part." Given all we know about even the best of intentions made on the basis of the best preparations, it is unreasonable and unrealistic to impose a solemn vow unto death upon what is arguably one of the most challenging of all relationships to maintain in peace and fulfillment. What should be asked of a couple is a fully informed intention to maintain and cultivate the marital state in which, at the time of their wedding, they ideally abide, and to seek the help of the congregation in doing so. Again, an ongoing program of marriage maintenance and enrichment ought to be the goal of every congregation. So, too, for couples who down the road suffer failure and possible dissolution of the marriage there should be a special counseling and referral program available, as well as a personal support network. Marriages that are saved and put on surer footing might, too, be appropriate subjects for blessing, celebration and recognition. It is no sin to fail or to fear failure. So it should be well within a congregation's responsibility to offer such a rite to couples whose marriage has been repaired and rejuvenated.

To return for a moment to the notion that marriage "signifies the union that exists between Christ and his church." Of the nearly 400 weddings at which I have officiated across 30 years, I know of no couple who ever took those words seriously. I never did, and all too recently I have omitted them from my reading of the service. The idea that in some sense the church is "the bride of Christ" cannot resonate with contemporary Christians who prize intellectual honesty. The phrase should be abandoned. And as to John's singular story of Jesus turning water into wine at a wedding in Cana, the less said about that the better.

A concluding word about the blessing of same-sex unions. While the term "marriage" is probably inappropriate to describe such unions, it is not to say that homosexual unions are in anyway inferior to their heterosexual counterparts. I disown my own Episcopal Church's continued disputations around this subject. Those who agree, as I do, that monogamous, faithful sexual unions — heterosexual and homosexual — are to be afforded equal standing need simply to ignore those church-types who continue to whine about "scriptural norms" and the sanctity of the family. The lasting homosexual unions about which I know partake of eros and agape in the same way as the lasting heterosexual unions I know. I know children who have been or are being raised by same-sex couples. Parenting, as it turns out, is parenting and two are better than one, the gender being less important than the number. In one such case, I am privileged to be the male-father role model for a daughter of a lesbian couple. That daughter and my own daughter are of an age and best friends.

All of which is to say that congregations who wish to live their lives as 21st-century people will want to tune out the noise of the unwinnable debate over whether gay and lesbian persons are fully human and arrange the order of their communities' lives in such a way as to welcome persons of either sexual orientation, holding all accountable for responsible and faithful conduct of their lives.

FUNERALS

More well-intentioned dishonesty is expressed in burial rites than in any other of the church's public services. Even in 1997 at my own aunt's funeral, the priest spoke glibly of heaven as if it were a superb five-star resort just around the bend in the road down which, of course, we're all merrily traveling. It's just that Rita Cameron got there ahead of us, so what are all these tears about? She's far better off where she is. The congregation drank it in as a desert wanderer would slake his thirst with a cup of cold water. When it was my turn to speak, I had to suppress the urge to say that my colleague was full of beans. It would have been merciless to do so. My cousins and my late aunt's aged friends had come to hear exactly what the priest had said, even though I am sure many of them knew it was all mental placebo.

To make over funeral rites for the 21st century will require a thorough rethinking and restatement of the church's teaching on the resurrection of Jesus upon which rests all that the kindly priest told my grieving family. I undertake that task earlier in this book and in an appendix yet to come, but I will summarize those efforts here.

The various incarnations of human belief about resurrection or immortality are certainly born of the natural denial that life will and must end for each of us. The basal instinct for self-preservation belies that denial. We really know it will end, we just want to postpone the ending of it as long as possible and to savor it while it is still good and we are able to enjoy it. Contrary to the epigrammatic proposition,

"Every good thing must come to an end," are the several human belief systems that posit one kind or another of deliverance from the grave and an eternal lasting of the self in some form. There is an undeniable germ of truth in that statement inasmuch as we are biochemical creatures, and while death does end the life of an individual as an individual, his/her remains in one way or another take different shapes, forms and substances in the biosphere. That, of course, is not enough for those who wish to understand their immortality in more personal terms.

To have thought of Jesus of Nazareth as anything less than personally resurrected would have been abhorrent to the survivors of his early first-century community. Those who later thought of him as christos, the eternal Son of God, had to find a new way to speak of him in absentia. Hence the doctrine of the particular physical resurrection of Jesus and, through Paul (see I Corinthians 15:12-28), the general resurrection. That has become the philosophical ground for most Christian burial rites. Nothing of an objectifiably attestable nature can be adduced to suggest that either resurrection or eternal life beyond the obvious decomposition and redistribution of bodily remains is reality, possibility or probability. Take away that from the burial rites, and what is left? Actually, a lot.

A funeral or burial rite needs to emphasize the exquisite nature of life itself, its preciousness that derives directly from its obvious finitude and the opportunity it affords to make a onetime difference for the living and as yet unborn. A funeral, of course, needs to honor the uniqueness of the one who has died, to celebrate his/her accomplishments and peculiarity or distinctiveness. Beyond that, a funeral is the context in which meaning is sought and conferred upon the circumstances of the death at hand.

A young father of small children who was making a name for himself in pioneering cancer research is struck and killed by a drunken driver. That is an example of the random nature of the universe in which such things are as likely as not to happen. Learning? "So teach us to number our days that we may get a heart of wisdom" (Psalm 90:12). Then what? Then the community is urged, even exhorted, to gather around the widow and her children to begin to bind up the broken hearts and repair the breach that has been so cruelly torn. Anything else? Yes, a redoubling of efforts in the community's formation program with regard to substance abuse and social responsibility. Perhaps the community as part of the funeral rite begins a project to memorialize the one who has died in some way commensurate with who and what he was, e.g., a college scholarship for his children, a fund to establish a program to aid the local government in treating those who have been convicted of drunken driving, an annual lectureship honoring the one who has died on developments in the area of his research.

All of these options focus on life — the past life of the deceased, the present life of his surviving family and the religious community of which they are a part and on the future of their lives and of the wider society.

Why is all that important? It is important because it is of the here and now that can be known, dealt with, believed and even believed in. It does not deal with the knowable and improbable and does not try to gloss over the sheer truth of the matter.

Certainly there may be resurrection and even eternal life. I would enthusiastically welcome both. Meanwhile, though, no reliable evidence suggests either might or even ought to be possibilities. Is it not better to deal with what seems to be true and does in fact happen than to draw the bereaved into temporary unreality for the sole purpose of anesthetizing them against the terrible pain that they must bear? The church's way-out-of-hand theology of resurrection and eternal life has become the substitute for human solidarity and comfort. Members of a community who have covenanted life together become instantly responsible as comforters and care-givers when death strikes. They should not rely on the clergy to find yet a new way to present the myth of the dying and rising god — and therefore of those who believe in him — as a means of comforting the bereaved but to be themselves the means of that comfort.

Death also occurs after considerable warning of its approach, say in the case of one who at six to nine months prior to the end is told by competent medical authorities that he or she is terminally ill. Now not only does the resurrection-eternal life business come into play but also the "miracle." Again, it is a natural part of the human denial of death's inevitability to hope for some miraculous turnaround in a hopelessly terminal situation. Yes, I have been witness to lives which have been prolonged and even enhanced by sheer exertion of the human will. Helen comes to mind. In her 70s she was diagnosed after exploratory surgery with advanced abdominal cancer. She refused to take that for an answer and fairly coerced physicians into a regime of chemotherapy which even they thought would be a waste of time and resources. She slogged through six months of chemotherapy with all its attendant miseries but emerged at the end of it bald but with her cancer in what was called "profound remission." She is careful not to commit the solipsism of "I prayed hard enough that God spared me" but chalked up her victory to her stubbornness, her husband's never-failing optimism and the advances of medical science. She also knows that, no matter what the cancer may do, she has lived most of her life.

Helen is, alas, the exception to the rule. What then to do when cancer really is terminal? The person who is terminal is helped by his/her family, with members of the community in close and active attendance, to accept the facts as they are. Then a plan is laid out for the final days, weeks and months — in a way similar to how a family would plan a special time together when all the kids are home from college or homes in other cities. Such a time is always an admixture of joy and sadness because, perforce, it must come to an end. So with the life of a terminally ill person and his/her family and greater community. One plans in the virtually sure and certain knowledge that the time is not only finite but measurable. That, of course, is a model for the living of anyone's life because one generally knows neither the day nor the hour.

What emphases, then, around the funeral rite for one whose death the community has known for some time was coming? Certainly a focus on moments in the intentional life which were planned and lived by the family of the deceased and the community in the weeks and months prior to the death. To recall and savor the good of that passage and to acknowledge the times of hurt and sadness that will undoubtedly have occurred will be as necessary.

The deceased will have comported himself/herself in such and such a way during the terminal days. Where such conduct has been heroic and worthy of note, this should be celebrated. There are always other heroes in such situations — physicians, other clinical or hospice care-givers, family, community members, neighbors, friends. At a funeral of that sort, acknowledgment of their ministries can be made and they may be asked to speak about their experiences and feelings. Add to that the honoring of the deceased and the celebration of his/her life accomplishments, and you have an affirmation of life as it has been lived and the conferring of meaning on a death that took its time in coming. Airy hopes of something else sometime, somewhere have been eschewed and intellectual honesty has been preserved. Reality has been noted and accepted. That would be a fitting epitaph for anyone.

Of the biblical literature that might be used in a funeral, these passages are among those that would work: the book of Job, Psalm 90, Ecclesiastes 3, Isaiah 40:1-8, Isaiah 55:6-13, Isaiah 61:1-4,

Jeremiah 32:6-15, Micah 6:6-8, Habakkuk 3:17-19, Matthew 5:1-12 (and other parallels as found), Matthew 13:1-9, Mark 12:41-44, 13:28-37, Luke 6:37-38, I Corinthians 13, I John 4:7-12. Obviously these passages will need analysis and interpretation by competent persons.

ORDINATION

Ordinations, and certainly those with which I am familiar in the Episcopal Church, resemble nothing so much as they resemble coronations. I remember my own now more than 30 years ago. I was the crown prince on whom the light had shone. I now had the faculties to make ordinary bread and wine into extraordinary bread and wine. I could confer blessings and absolve penitents of their sins. Or so it was said and believed by enough people to make it so.

It has taken a long time for me to appreciate how that ecclesiology-demonstrated-in-liturgy distorts the meaning of ordained ministry for which the model must surely be something similar to what is reported in various Christian texts about Jesus of Nazareth calling this one and that one into a tough and demanding discipleship, the destination of which can range anywhere from deprivation to death. It has nothing to do with the accumulation of power or its use to dominate anyone. The ordained ministry has unfortunately been an agency of domination and misuse of power since the inception of the idea that human beings could be intermediaries between the gods and fellow humans.

In the 21st-century church or religious community, the "who's in charge?" question will eventually be answered by individual local communities. And the answer will be "We are." As that development evolves there will be less and less reliance on bishops, superintendents, dioceses and synods and also less attention paid to them. American Roman Catholicism since the mid-1960s has been something of a model for decentralization as more clergy, religious and laity consider the Vatican Curia and the pope as irrelevant to the practice of religion. Eventually as the trend to decentralization continues, the meaning of ordination will come into question and significant changes will occur.

The Lutherans have it about right with their bishoprics being not only elective but with term limits as well. One does not become bishop for life as in the Roman Catholic, Anglican and Orthodox communities, but for a stated time. In that spirit, perhaps congregations will have a greater and greater say in who their ordained leadership will be and on what terms. The Congregational Church more or less provides a model for this — albeit a flawed one — as do most Conservative and Reform Jewish synagogues whose rabbis serve under contracts with lay boards and more or less at their pleasure. But term limits for leadership and at-will employment are not exactly the direction communities will want to take. The model of Mutual Ministry which is under experimental use in areas of the Episcopal Church, and by different names in other religious communities, places emphasis on a local community's discernment of who their own leaders really are in a given time and situation and raising them up for ordination for local ministry only. Yet in the Episcopal Church at least there still exists the doctrine of the indelibility of orders, thus creating a permanent and distinct class of persons. And even in the Mutual Ministry model, ordination is conferred by an authority outside the community. This is due in part to the way most every denomination prepares and educates its ordained leadership, viz., in seminaries or theological colleges, thus producing an elite, the members of which will inevitably identify with one another — a kind of guild or professional association. Such a bonding is natural, even inevitable, though it ends up creating authority problems in the local community. The way most denominations do business, the senior minister, pastor or rector is to one degree or another selected by a remote authority or elected from a pool of applicants vetted by such an authority. The one appointed or elected almost always comes from the outside. There is conferred thereby an instant authority upon that person which he/she has not earned and which, in fact, he/she will really not possess in any effective way until such time as the community itself sees fit to confer it. Any bishop, superintendent, synod president or conference minister could tell hair-raising stories about how that kind of system can and does backfire. Conflict resolution efforts abound, all meant to repair the damage that occurs as trust is never built, authority is misused or when mismatches occur.

Perhaps a more workable system for 21st-century religious communities could put what we now call sacramental, pastoral and administrative authority and responsibility entirely under local control, leaving to the adult participating members the process of discerning who in a given time and under given conditions ought to be recruited and empowered as leaders. In almost any circumstance one can think of, the person or persons who are raised up to be liturgical presidents should have the trust of the community, should be, as it were, model citizens and possess the kind of personal authority and composure that fit them to lead others. A ceremony formally to confer such term-limited authority could be both profound and simple, a traditional laying-on-of-hands, the ceremonial presentation of common-meal vessels or other paraphernalia associated with the community's liturgical life.

Pastoral leaders need to possess special skills, or those deemed most fit to lead pastoral initiatives and responses may be sent for training — even to earn degrees. Such pastoral figures would need to be perceived almost universally within the community as possessing great discretion, common wisdom and emotional accessibility. They would ideally be characterized, in the words of the late Edwin Friedman, "non-anxious presences." Also ideally they would have been members of the community for some time and be well-known by all.

Indeed, pastoral leaders could almost be interchangeable with liturgical leaders, except the decentralization of authority and responsibility is a desirable goal.

Again, the formal conferring of pastoral responsibility can take the form of a commissioning, in which the congregational roll or directory including photos of all members and their brief histories are presented to those selected. A list of community members currently in crisis might also be part of the presentation to be followed by a laying-on-of-hands or other symbolic action commensurate with a setting-apart.

Administrative responsibilities will be conferred upon persons of great and proven probity and skill who will function in collegiality with the community's elected board or council. Administrators can be recognized and their appointment concurred in by the community as such obvious symbols of administrative responsibility as keys, ledgers and bank books are presented.

The process of selecting, recruiting, training and commissioning of these three categories of ministers is left to the local community with the advice of annual reviews of the conduct of their ministries on behalf of the congregation and periodic reselection or election of others so that a) power does not for the long term become concentrated among a few and b) all participating adult members can share authority and responsibility over time, making for a stronger and more vital community.

The one ministry remaining is that of education. And here's where what are now known as professional clergy enter the picture — except they will be academicians not ecclesiastical technicians. One of the big mistakes most denominations have made is the development of professional clergy — men and women who may or may not have earned a professional degree on par with that of a dental surgeon, physician, clinical psychologist or attorney, a degree that for all intents and purposes allows one to practice a certain field. For clergy with professional degrees that commonly means practicing in a wide-open, general field involving public speaking, teaching, pastoral care, administration and liturgy. A three-year professional degree cannot really prepare the average person to do all of that well — which is why so many ordained clergy appear to be marginal or, at worst, incompetent. To be all the things that clergy are expected to be in congregations of more than 100-200 members in truth would require (or ought to) at least a normal baccalaureate degree plus a B.S. in business, an M.A. in psychology and no less than a master's level degree in religion. But even that field is broad including, fundamentally, comparative religions, Old and New Testament studies, history, philosophy and theology. Few if any persons can come close to mastering more than one, at best two, of those areas. The ideal would be to earn a Ph.D. in one of those dominant fields with extra work in one or two related fields. With the kind of system in place as described above, a person now called a professional minister would be free ab initio from pastoral, liturgical and administrative work to be the resident academician.

So the proposal is for associations of local communities to recruit from among the superior graduates of good liberal arts colleges or universities men and women who can and will go on to reputable graduate schools of religion, to obtain Ph.D.s in one or another of the major fields — biblical studies being the much preferred one, though a doctoral degree in any one of the major fields makes its recipient well-qualified to teach undergraduates or their equivalent in related fields as often happens at the collegiate level.

A community and others with which it may be associated would need to raise the funds necessary to aid Ph.D. candidates in return for their agreement to become scholars-in-residence for some minimum term of years at a salary commensurate with their counterparts at small to medium-sized colleges. Opportunities and funds for postdoctoral research would have to be provided.

The responsibilities of the community's scholar-in-residence would include oversight of the education program in all its aspects, including recruitment and training of teachers, teaching a regular load (three) of classes per term (three annually) for members of the community at the lower undergraduate level and, over time, beyond. Class topics would include Old and New Testament studies, comparative religion, philosophy of religion, systematic and historical theology, ethics and church history.

The scholar-in-residence might also be competent at least to advise and instruct pastoral and liturgical ministers. He/she would have the option of becoming a full member of the community but not eligible to become a liturgical, pastoral or administrative minister — again the concern being the diffusion and decentralization of authority and responsibility.

I would strongly recommend against any ordination-like or even commissioning ritual for the scholar-in-residence because his/her authority derives from the faculty that conferred the degree and from the regimen by and through which it was earned. The scholar-in-residence would be exactly that and not a minister or leader with local authority.

* * *

The rites and responsibilities I have herein envisioned for a new kind of religious congregation of the 21st century describe a community that would be truly egalitarian and democratic with power and authority shared at all times by all adult members, making all of them "ministers" or, as the Latin derivative of that word means, "servants," but servants each to all and all to each with authority conferred (and

69

removed) by the collective will of the community. I do not expect to see the realization of this vision in my lifetime. It came to me much too late in a professional clergy career now dependent on denominational support, pensions and benefits. If I were 10 years younger and of independent means — or single without children — I would try to found such a community as I have herein described and to work with like-minded persons to establish the rites and responsibilities I have set forth provisionally. Circumstances, however, dictate that some one else to whom these ideas and proposals seem interesting and worth a try will feel free to appropriate, amend, alter and certainly improve upon them. He or she may feel equally free to claim all credit, because it would all be much easier said than done.

Mine has been a long and sometimes difficult journey, beginning in small-town Protestantism, with two separate and quite different sojourns in the Episcopal Church which bookended a serious flirtation with Roman Catholicism. As I will describe in some detail later in this book, all the while a strong agnostic strain has marked all my searchings. Through a chance meeting with Rabbi Sherwin T. Wine of Farmington Hills, Michigan, many years ago, an inner light was kindled in me that took years to burn at sufficient strength to show the way. Rabbi Wine is a pioneer in cultural humanistic Judaism and, as such, helped reinvent a traditional expression of religion into a relevant, intellectually honest and utterly usable movement. Rabbi Wine and those who have followed him have discovered a wealth of Jewishness among the welter of theistic texts, ideas and dogma. They have figured out how to celebrate their Jewishness without the baggage of shopworn theology and largely meaningless ritual. It is, of course, a relatively small movement because it has removed the "bankies" and the pacifiers from the crib, and has, in fact, removed the rails from the crib and invited adult infants to get up and out.

Rabbi Wine and his fellow humanistic Jews have been denounced for years as apostates. That, of course, was inevitable. The vitriol has largely gone out of the criticism, however, though the Generation X Jews seem to be flocking back to the more traditional communities. That should not discourage humanist Jews, and it should not discourage those who would consider seriously the proposals included in this book. Pendula shift with the passage of time and the change of circumstance. There will always be a place for an agnostic, rational and humanistic appreciation and application of religion. There are those who will always need it for a refuge of intellectual honesty as they make their way through the Persian bazaar of cant, hypocrisy, uncritical tradition and dogma which all too frequently characterize religion and its institutions.

PRAYER

What is absent from the proposed, experimental rites discussed earlier is the mention of prayer, which accounts for so much of the content of the rites and rituals of most Christian communities. That absence is an intended one. To pray is to posit a personal god who can and presumably will hear the content of one's prayer and perhaps even respond to the petition, confession or intercession. What observable or even inferable data can be put forward to suggest that such a proposition is more than fantasy or wishful thinking? This is not to say that there may not be such a god as traditional Christianity envisions, so this is not atheism. It is agnosticism. An agnostic says, "I don't know." Whether or not we own up to it, we are all agnostics where "God" is concerned. One may hope God as variously envisioned actually is; one may believe that a god is; one cannot know it. If reason and experience are the means by which human beings agree that something is so (e.g., the Earth revolves around a star known as the Sun), then it is impossible to say "I know that God hears prayer."

In a community that wishes its rites to be based on reason and to have them bespeak intellectual honesty and realism, prayer as we know it needs to be forgone. What to put in its place? A passage from the gospel called "According to John" suggests what "prayer" might be to the 21st-century congregation. John 17:1-11 is a portion of what is known as Jesus' High Priestly prayer. One must remember that John has previously depicted Jesus as being one with the logos ("And the Word was with God and the Word was God"). In that sense, Jesus would have been talking to himself.

A contemporary congregation might be better off spending its time and resources talking to itself — members talking with and listening to other members — than in addressing an unseen god which may or may not be or which may be inaccessible to human beings. Again, this is not an appeal to atheism but to agnosticism. Talking earnestly and listening carefully with and to one another in the spirit of Jesus whose ethical teachings govern a community's conduct might be an acceptable substitute for prayer. Such talking and listening can, if intentional and grounded in trust, prove to be a process of discernment, which, after all, is what prayer is.

Paul Tillich's signal contribution to religious thought was the concept of the uncreated creator. Tillich once responded to a graduate student's question, "Does God exist?" with a monosyllabic, "Nein!" For Tillich, what some call "God" was not a being nor yet being at all but "the ground and source of being." If communication or communion with God is sought, Tillich would have one consult any of the forms of being that abound in the known universe for clues as to God's will, plan, intention, whatever. Moreover, the Episcopal Book of Common Prayer (page 323), following the concept of Psalm 139:1-3 envisions a God "unto whom all hearts are open, all desires known, and from whom no secrets are hid." If that piece of theology resonates with members of a congregation, they might be willing to content themselves with speaking, listening, reflecting and doing as if, or in the belief that, god or God is totally aware of their common life and through one or more of them from time to time attempting to affect it.

Classic analyses of prayer include the subtypes of praise, confession, petition, intercession and thanksgiving. Within the rubrics of reason, how can those forms be retained and altered to suit the 20th-century church?

What is at the heart of the worship or praise of an unseen power? The Webster's Ninth New Collegiate dictionary defines worship as "reverence paid to a divine being." Tillich would say to "the ground and source of being." In more primitive times what is now called worship was certainly thought to be appeasement of the unseen but surely mighty and fearsome forces that caused floods, fires, damaging winds, famine, ailments, suffering and death. A touch of that carried over into pre-Vatican II Roman Catholicism as the laity were taught that missing mass on required days of obligation was a sin for which one needed to make an act of contrition, else one's soul was not in a state of grace. I trust it is not too much to expect that a good many people are beyond that point and that worship, so-called, is understood to be a voluntary, discretionary act to be offered in freedom and apart from institutional coercion.

What might be an acceptable form of praise or thanksgiving for a 21st-century Christian community? There is an abundance of natural phenomena ranging all the way from the life-hospitable climate of our planet to the human capacities to think, remember, reflect, care and love. In between are the glories of nature, the gifts of music and the arts, the monumental achievements of human history, the everyday pleasures of living and loving and the opportunities given us for service to others. Prose, poetry and musical compositions are appropriate resources for the gathering up of human awe and gratitude — works that are agnostic as to the cause-and-effect factor of the universe and its multitudinous creatures. As an example, this passage from William Wordsworth's "Tintern Abbey:"

"For I have learned
To look on nature, not as in the hour
Of thoughtless youth; but hearing oftentimes
The still, sad music of humanity,
Nor harsh, nor grating, though of ample power
To chasten and subdue. And I have felt
A presence that disturbs me with the joy
Of elevated thoughts; a sense sublime
Of something far more deeply interfused,
Whose dwelling is the light of setting suns,
And the round ocean and the living air,
And the blue sky, and in the mind of man;
A motion and a spirit that impels
All thinking objects, all objects of all thought,
And rolls through all things. Therefore am I still
A lover of the meadows and the woods,
And mountains; and of all the mighty world
Of eye, and ear, — both what they half create
And what perceive; well pleased to recognise
In nature and the language of the sense,
The anchor of my purest thoughts, the nurse,
The guide, the guardian of my heart, and soul
Of all my moral being."

Such literature is uplifting, honest and honoring of the ambiguity that so enshrouds human thinking and intuition about those questions for which there exist no answers. Wordsworth's words from the late 18th century would well serve a 21st-century congregation in its desire to celebrate and give thanks for the gifts of life.

Prayers of confession to an unseen deity are exercises in avoidance. One does wrong to other people individually or collectively.

The devastating put-down needs to be atoned for by sincere apology to the one put down. A generation's profligacy where the use of fossil fuels is concerned needs to be atoned for in direct action aimed at reducing such use and eradicating as much as possible its ill effects. In other words, confession is a matter not largely of talk but of action. Paradoxically, the authors of the classic Roman Catholic-Anglican orders for Reconciliation of a Penitent grasped the importance of human interaction in what is called confession. Required by Rome but optional for Anglicans is the custom of making a confession to a priest who, representing the church and God, hears out a penitent, prescribes penance and amendment of life and in most cases pronounces absolution, which is contingent upon the carrying out of the assigned penance and amendment. Contrition in a 21st-century religious community will involve open and honest discussion of individual and corporate wrongdoing and an appreciation of how wrongs can be righted. How each community does that will be its call, and natural forms will evolve for local use.

Prayers of petition are direct requests to a deity perceived by the prayer to be powerful enough to grant them. "Give us this day our daily bread." What if a starving one in the famine-stricken Sudan utters that prayer in expectation that his child's distended stomach will finally be filled, only to see that child die before his very eyes? What will that petitioner come to believe of the deity he trusted to give that day's crucial bread? Despite the frequent witnesses to the proposition that "God answers prayers," there daily remain millions of unanswered prayers. The picture that paints of the kind of deity such prayers envision is ludicrous. Were it to exist, such a deity would be capricious, cruel and judgmental in the extreme. Who but the psychologically warped wishes to have anything to do with such a deity or notion of it?

Especially noxious are those who purvey the religion of success.

"If you pray hard enough and send in your prayer offering, your prayer will be answered and you will become rich beyond measure." The sad fact of the matter is that thousands upon thousands of people have fallen for such scams but remain believers nonetheless. How does one become wealthy? Mostly by betting on the right horse, buying the right lottery ticket, being smart in business or profession, by saving every single discretionary dime and wisely investing it or by inheriting wealth from a relative or friend. If there are other ways, besides bank robbery or embezzlement, to get rich, I do not know of them. Prayers of petition to a perceived deity avail nothing of material wealth.

Asking a deity for wisdom, guidance, direction or insight seems on the face of it to be an exercise in humility and infinitely preferable to asking for wealth. But what do those who make such prayers really expect? Certainly not a divine whisper in the ear or handwriting on the wall or an angelic visitation. When the governing board of the congregation I serve meets to do business, it is customary and expected that I, as pastor, will open the meeting with a prayer for guidance. I oblige, but what I am really doing in the hushed atmosphere that usually greets prayer's onset is laying out the method we have previously agreed will lead us to consensus. "Let us listen to one another with open minds, attentive to the trust we have built among ourselves. Let us see as much of the whole picture of a thing as we can. Let us be ever mindful of the responsibilities we have agreed to discharge." Some may think of such words as being addressed to a deity. They leave my lips as reminders to all of us present of how we have intended to do business. If the ground and source of being is aware of my words and is moved in some way to help us, I would be surprised to know it but altogether grateful for it.

Intercessory prayer is about as radical an act as I can think of. Given a deity of the kind that is supposed by conventional religion to exist, what can it mean for one to petition it on behalf of another who either doesn't know or doesn't want what the intercessor wants. I am unhappily reminded of an incident of a number of years ago when I was with a member of my congregation who, while still conscious, was within hours of dying and was praying that death might come sooner rather than later. While I stayed out of the praying, I certainly did offer a robust "Amen" to his prayer. Come to find out, several members of his family were in an anteroom praying in intercession that he would not die but await some divine miracle or sensational new medical discovery. This occurred at the time the tune "Dueling Banjos" was all the rage, and the tune would not leave my head as, alternately, I heard diametrically opposing and competing prayers. It was then that I figured out for myself that, if a deity — or Tillich's ground of being — is aware of human prayer, such a deity must be immensely amused and tolerant of its naivete and desperation. The crudely expressed bumper-sticker wisdom to the effect that things happen is about how it is and will be. Thus I wonder that people do not spend the time and energy devoted to intercessory prayer in helping those concerned prepare for whatever inevitability is about to come and talk to each other about how to accomplish what needs doing or will need to be done.

Surely we do not believe that a deity worthy of human trust would grant one prayer and not another, would allow one terminally ill sufferer to die and another miraculously to live. Religious people need to intercede with and for one another when the going gets rough. And, again, if a deity or a "ground of being" — call it what you will — is out there, aware and sympathetic, swell. If not, we need to carry on, drawing on the considerable resources of the human mind and spirit to ease suffering and give care and comfort.

Part Three:
The Bible Without Creeds

This section will consist in a series of analyses of New Testament texts in rational and Enlightenment, rather than dogmatic and traditional, terms. They may not be the best or the clearest things of their kind, but they represent what in a post-credal church may take the place of excessively right-brained hortatory sermons. While most of the interpretations originated with the author, standard commentaries were consulted along with many of the sources cited by the authors and editors of the commentaries.

Volumes VIII and IX of *The New Interpreter's Bible* were consulted along with the *Anchor Bible* series on Matthew (W.F. Albright and C.S. Mann), Mark (C.S. Mann), Luke (Joseph A. Fitzmyer) and John (Raymond E. Brown); Rudolf Bultmann's seminal *The Gospel According to John;* Chad Myers' *Binding the Strong Man* (a commentary on Mark); Burton Mack's *The Lost Gospel,* and John Kloppenborg's *The Formation of Q.* As background, I used Brown's *Death of the Messiah* with further help from John Dominic Crossan's *The Historical Jesus,* Bernard Brandon Scott's *Hear Then the Parable* and John P. Meier's *A Marginal Jew*. The author's own translations, analyses and exegetical notes accumulated over 30 years of study and research were also employed.

MATTHEW 2:1-12

The story of the Magi which makes this day (Epiphany) is unique to Matthew and has no other direct allusions in scripture. In formulating the story, Matthew may very well have had both Isaiah 60:6 and Psalm 72:11 and 15a in mind if, indeed, he did not actually incorporate their imagery with his penchant for fulfillment texts, along with the quotation he lifted from Zechariah 9:9. So the question that must be asked is, "What place in Matthew's program does this obviously fabricated story occupy?"

Consider the situation in Matthew's community — perhaps in Antioch of Syria ca. 75-85 C.E. He was surrounded by Jewish Christians of the second generation still with an institutional memory of the Judaism their forbearers had known and practiced — a generation of converts who were perhaps having second thoughts about their conversion, wondering if Jesus was the messiah and, if so, where was he and where was the supposed glory of the messianic age?

The story of the Magi is preceded by Matthew's creative account of Jesus' origins (1:18-25), in which Jesus is said to be the son of God by the intervention of "the Most High" who effects Jesus' conception in his mother's womb. This is to establish Jesus as the anointed one — anointed even before birth. And if that was not convincing enough for his Jewish-Christian congregation, Matthew reaches further into his imagination and creates the magi and their pilgrimage to worship a newborn king. Give Matthew an A for effort!

Jews are depicted in their history as owing something of their national existence to a Persian king who put pressure on his vassal state of Babylon to free exiled Jews ca. 545 B.C.E., thus paving the way for the restoration and rebuilding of the Temple and its society.

The story of the magi, who would have been understood by first-century hearers as astrologers of the royal house of Persia, coming a great distance to worship the King of the Jews would turn the tables. In 545 B.C.E., the second Isaiah called Cyrus the Lord's anointed (45:1). Now guess who's the anointed? A new "king" being honored by remnants of the Persian house.

With this story, Matthew makes Israel and the Jews the center of the world instead of a marginalized and insignificant people and so cleverly ties together Jewish tradition and the proclamation of Jesus as messiah. The significance of this story, however fabricated it is, is not to be discounted. Matthew means by it to say that Jesus of Nazareth (by Matthew's time Jesus proclaimed as resurrected) had significance beyond the borders of Judaism as one who represented in his ethical and wisdom teachings — many of which Matthew will go on to incorporate into his gospel — something universal and in some way connected to the world as its source/orderer may want it to be.

MATTHEW 3:13-17

Who chose Jesus to be "the Son of God?" The obvious answer is God, but it seriously begs the question if only because that simply cannot be known in any objectifiable or verifiable way — especially if the idea of "God" is also not objectifiable or verifiable but rather a matter of subjectivity.

Looking back to the second Isaiah (42:1ff), we see the prophet singling out Israel as Jahweh's chosen servant who is to be a bringer of justice. So for time out of mind the Jews have thought of themselves as the chosen people. After Auschwitz and Buchenwald, it is necessary to ask, "Chosen for what?"

Meanwhile, it is fair to say that the sixth-century B.C.E. writer Isaiah did the choosing of his own people in declaring that Jahweh had set them apart for a special mission. Then we come to Jesus of Nazareth who, it is manifestly obvious to anyone who reads the New Testament, was chosen messiah by its authors and the communities in which their writings were shaped. Whoever Jesus was revealed to be by his ethical and wisdom teaching was what Jahweh looked like to them.

Ever since, Christian communities in every age have chosen Jesus, too, if not as messiah at least as one who mediates useful truth. What complicates matters for this simple statement is that the synoptic gospels depict God as having chosen Jesus in a very public way: "And just as he was coming up out of the water, he saw the heavens torn apart and the Spirit descending like a dove on him, and a voice came from heaven said, 'You are my son, the Beloved; with you I am well pleased' " (Mark 1:10-11 with parallels in Matthew 3: 16-17 and Luke 3: 21-22).

As long as we understand that the gospels were written 30 to 60 years after the events they supposedly depict and that they were meant not to inform but to persuade, it is then possible and desirable to establish that Mark (and after him Matthew and Luke) chose Jesus — not John the Baptist, not the mythic son of Mithra or others he might have chosen to declare God's son, but Jesus. That is an important distinction to make in a world of fomenting fundamentalisms in which each insists loudly and threateningly that its way is the only way. The international nightmares of Iran, Libya and Algeria and American's own Christian right and its constituent parts come alarmingly to mind. If it is necessary for Christians to say "Jesus is the one," let them say so by living out his ethical and wisdom teaching and let those with whom they live decide if their example suggests that they're on to something.

Who says "Jesus is the one?" We do, and we could be wrong in the long term, in the bigger picture we cannot see. But trying to be faithful doesn't necessarily mean being right. Martin Buber, in an

81

address to Roman Catholic priests given at a time Jews and Catholics did not talk much, set down a fine standard by which proponents of any religion may judge themselves and their zeal to lay claim to truth: "What is the difference between Jews and Christians? We all await the messiah. You believe he has already come and gone, while we do not. I therefore propose that we await him together. And when he appears we can ask him, 'Were you here before?' And I hope that at that moment I will be close enough to whisper in his ear, 'For the love of heaven, don't answer.' "

MATTHEW 5:21-48

"But I say to you that if you are angry with a brother or sister, you will be liable to judgment." Who would want to live in a world in which bad thoughts (not even carried out) and in which the expression of anger would be tickets to eternal damnation? You? Not me! Who has never harbored a dark thought toward another, has not lusted in the imagination or lost his or her temper? How then appropriate this difficult passage?

To help us, there are a few things New Testament studies have helped bring to light:

a) Matthew, whoever he was, had a delicate balancing act to perform between Jewish converts to Christianity and Gentile aspirants who were strangers to Torah. Matthew had to keep Torah in place and at the same time help both strangers and longtime adherents to see it in a new light. So there is ambiguity present in his gospel, for example: Matthew begins the gospel by depicting Joseph as acting other than the law provided in declining to divorce his pregnant betrothed but to marry her instead. Is this Matthew's nuanced hint that there is a higher authority than the law?

b) Matthew evidently believed Jesus was not only the fulfillment but the perfection of the law and so included in his account this saying attributed to Jesus: "You have heard it said, 'An eye for an eye, and a tooth for a tooth' (Exodus 21:24, Leviticus 24:20), but I say to you, if anyone strikes you on the right cheek, turn the other also"; and this: "You have heard it said, 'You shall love your neighbor and hate your enemy,' but I say to you, love your enemies"; and this: "The son of Man is Lord of the sabbath" elsewhere expressed as "the sabbath was made for human kind, not human kind for the sabbath."

Matthew brackets this whole section on the law with these memorable words: "In everything, do to others as you would have them do to you; for this is the law and the prophets" (7:12). Even as Matthew seems to be saying that unexpressed anger will bring the law's judgment, he is softening already actual statutes: "You have heard ... but I tell you."

If one is in the habit of entertaining bad thoughts and evil intentions toward others, he or she is likely to speak out from time to time in anger. Such behavior, given human nature, is likely to feed on itself, creating more bad thoughts and impulses of anger and to give occasion for both to be acted out. I offer Bosnia, Rwanda, Burundi and the intifada as examples.

Matthew said that Jesus entered the public sphere as the fulfillment and perfection of Torah, i.e., to give a human personality to the doing of the undoable. There is no doubt whatsoever that Jesus was thoroughly human, which is not to speak ill of him. But it is to say that if, indeed, he enjoined anger, he also became angry himself. Sixteen chapters hence in Matthew he will be depicted as having a terrible fit of temper as he overturned the tables of the cash exchangers and the chairs of the dove salesmen.

A world in which no bad thoughts or anger would exist is an impossibility, as both Jesus and Matthew surely knew. What, then, with this final demand that Matthew and Matthew alone among New Testament writers put on the lips of Jesus: "Be perfect, therefore, as your heavenly father is perfect"? "Perfect" is not the most helpful translation of the Greek *teleios*. I translate it "finished" or "mature," as in "be mature ones." BE GROWN UP! may be a fair interpretation. If we all acted in grown-up ways, not trying to outdo or put down one another, eschewing anger and disciplining our intentions and feelings and covenanting not to act out the antisocial ones, then perhaps the society that can be inferred from Jesus' ethical and wisdom teachings may actually to a significant degree be realized.

JOHN 4:7-30

To appreciate the full effect of this story about Jesus and the woman at the well, that is, the effect it would have had upon first-century Palestinian Jews, one would need to imagine what the general reaction of contemporary Christians would be to using churches in off-hours for "adult" entertainment purposes, or sanctuaries for political resistance, or sacred vessels for ordinary household purposes, or making public sexual intercourse as part of an initiation rite. In any of these cases, certain important boundaries would be crossed and customs seriously violated. In this passage from the Fourth Gospel, there are reported several boundary crossings:

1) Jesus crossed the border from Judea into Samaria on his way to Galilee instead of taking the more politically correct route up the Jordan River bank *around* Samaria. This is important because Samaria and its inhabitants were to Judeans repellant untouchables. Centuries before, the occupants of Samaria declared Mt. Gerizim — rather than Jerusalem — to be the true dwelling place of Jahweh and built a temple to that belief. Thus were borders and boundaries established.

2) Once across the border, Jesus is depicted as going to the well for a drink — a Samaritan well, mind you — and a well not belonging to him or to his tribe.

3) He is depicted as striking up a conversation with a woman, a woman who is a Samaritan; he endures her initial mockery of him — treating a woman as an equal, treating a Samaritan as an equal and begging a boon of her.

Here we pause to ask why John would go to the trouble of telling a story that will offend virtually all concerned? John has already identified Jesus not only as the long-awaited messiah of his people but the very logos in human figure — quite enough to alienate Jews. But now John is saying that this divine-human person pays no heed to borders or sociopolitical boundaries. The clear inference waiting to be made is that, for John, the logos neither recognizes nor respects borders and boundaries. The implication is that those who would join the Jesus movement shouldn't either.

We tend in this time to narrower and narrower definitions of who *we* are. We tend more and more to live behind fences, gates, walls and bars. We take refuge more and more in clan, sect, cult, kith and kin. Conversely, the picture of Jesus walking across the border into Samaria and all that is depicted as following from it is an invitation to us to do the same in our own way and time.

LUKE 24:13-35

The American poet Robert Frost wrote:

"Two roads diverged in a yellow wood
And sorry I could not travel both
and be one traveler
Long I stood and looked down one
as far as I could to where it bent in the undergrowth."

A road figures prominently in this gospel passage. It is the familiar road to Emmaus along which Luke alone among New Testament writers tells us that a disciple of Jesus named Cleopas and an unnamed companion walked and encountered a stranger who turned out to be

Jesus — only this was supposedly after Jesus' death. "Emmaus" — the word means "warm wells" or maybe "hot springs" — is mentioned in the Bible only here. No one knows where or if Emmaus might have been. Luke says Emmaus was 160 stadia, or about seven miles, from Jerusalem. There today in a westerly direction is a village called El-Qubelieh which the Romans of the first century called "Castellus Emmaus." To it even today exists a road from Jerusalem, and it is upon that road or one like it that we are asked to imagine Cleopas and his companion walking. In the process of that seven-mile journey — probably taking the better part of a day considering the terrain — Cleopas and his friend meet, converse with and finally recognize Jesus who is supposed to be dead and, eventually, vanishes as if he had not been there at all.

Luke wrote about another road, that in Acts of the Apostles 9:1-9 — but a much longer one spanning the distance from Judea to Damascus. Paul is portrayed as having traveled most of that distance on his way to investigating synagogues there and to expel from them those who might be agents provocateur for the Jesus movement. Unlike Cleopas and his friend who are depicted by Luke as wondering what had become of Jesus, Paul was all for stamping out any thought or memory of him. That, at least, is how Luke paints the picture though Paul himself in his extant correspondence gives no such account. What Luke asks us to picture is that, while on the way to Damascus, Paul is suddenly arrested by an intense light and hears the voice of Jesus long since dead. So shocked by this encounter was Paul that he was blinded for three days. In due course, he regained his composure and submitted himself to the movement he had been trying to stamp out.

It seems clear that both the Emmaus and the Damascus roads stories are confections, and we are pretty sure they are from the same pen. What then was Luke reacting to in the Christian communities out of which his gospel came? He was certainly seeing conversion going on around him as Jew and Gentile, coming down different roads on different journeys, were warming up to Jesus' ethical and wisdom teachings — suggesting that there is no one road to conversion and that, whatever road one takes, it goes ever, ever on. Just as Cleopas and friend left Emmaus and moved on, just as Paul left the place where his experience occurred, so contemporary Christians need to be on the move, on the road, evolving, becoming.

"Two roads diverged in a yellow wood
And sorry I could not travel both
and be one traveler.
Long I stood and looked down one
as far as I could to where it bent in the undergrowth.

"And both that morning equally lay
In leaves no step had trodden black.
Oh, I kept the first for another day!
Yet knowing how way leads on to way,
I doubted if I should ever come back."

MARK 1:1-15

Mark, whoever he was (and we are presuming it was "he"), was a literary pioneer. As the apocalyptic end of Jewish life in Palestine approached with the final siege of Jerusalem and its Temple, a new necessity was laid upon those who had made themselves responsible for preserving and enhancing the memory of Jesus. From the time of Jesus' death to the onset of the final days (a period of about 35 years), it seems that people remembered and maybe even worshiped Jesus through the repetition of certain of his pithy, countercultural sayings — for example, "Let the dead bury their dead," or "How fortunate are the hungry, they shall be fed," or "Love your enemies," or "Don't be afraid of those who can kill the body, but can't kill the soul." But the sayings of a rabbi from another generation were not sufficient to sustain the communities of Palestinian Jews, being that life as they had known it was coming to a fiery and bloody end. Inspirational literature of a different sort was needed. And so, drawing on the form of the ancient Greek heroic saga, a person in the Jewish community in Capernaum (others say in Rome) wrote what came to be called "a gospel," a proclamation of the good news.

This document was attributed to a writer named "Mark." Its appearance apparently had a stunning affect on other Jewish communities as well as on the Gentile world. It was soon being widely imitated and even copied with adaptations by other authors/editors, including some with the names of Matthew, Luke and John. Mark had included a number of the earlier sayings along with a whole corpus of new stories and narratives.

While the gospel according to Mark is in many ways similar to those that followed on his own and quoting at length from it, Mark is unique in that it does not include a post-resurrection experience, but rather leaves the reader with the words of "a young man dressed in white" who tells the women who have come to anoint Jesus' body for burial that "he has been raised." It has been pretty much determined by New Testament scholars over the past 150 years or so that the authentic Gospel of Mark ends with the eighth verse of the 16th chapter, which reads:

"So they went out from the tomb, for terror and amazement had seized them; and they said nothing to anyone, for they were afraid." The real climax of Mark, to which everything from Chapter 1/verse 1 leads, comes at the end of the crucifixion narrative (at Chapter 15, verse 39) when the centurion — one who, Mark wants us to understand, participated in Jesus' crucifixion — says at the moment of Jesus' death, "Surely this man was God's Son!"

This suggests strongly that Mark believed it was in Jesus'

suffering and death that he became divine. What an appropriate message to proclaim to a beleaguered and persecuted people whose life was chaos and whose hopes for survival were slim to none! Mark was telling them that suffering and death can give momentous meaning to life — maybe even meaning of deeper significance than merely living. That is the legacy which Mark brought to and left with early Christianity, and it resonates to this day.

ACTS 1:1-14

What has been traditionally termed "the Feast of the Ascension" has to do with the relationship the early Christian communities figured out they had with the one whose teaching had given them birth. Over time, those early communities gradually became reconciled to Jesus' death and began to build around it a truth-based legend having to do with the rejection Jesus may have experienced personally but certainly, too, the rejection to which his teachings were subjected even posthumously. The way the gospel story seems to have developed, Jesus was made to take on the characteristics of the suffering servant as depicted in the writings of the sixth-century B.C.E. Isaiah. These sufferings led to a death Christians came to believe had significance beyond the obvious. Meanwhile, the theme of resurrection was being added to the tradition as second and third generations of Christians began to believe that Jesus, whom they had never seen nor heard, was present among them.

When that belief was taken literally, almost surely there arose the problem of why no one could see Jesus if he was, indeed, alive. The Hellenistic concept of the heavenly realm was again drawn into the essentially earthbound Hebraic belief system. To answer the question of why nobody could see Jesus, the community said that, because he had come from God, he had been taken back to God and therefore into heaven and that, because he promised to be with them in any event (Matthew 28:20), his spirit lived on in the communities dedicated to him. This classic teaching of his ascension into heaven is of use only metaphorically. It is one way of saying that we want to believe that what Jesus represented by way of his ethical and wisdom teachings is somehow at or near the heart of the universe. And if our desire translates into acting on and acting out those teachings, the part of the world in which we live can only be the better for it.

JOHN 17:11-19

Jesus, as depicted by the author of the Fourth Gospel, says in what is known as his great High Priestly prayer that his followers "do not belong to this world." What could that mean? They were not, in so far as we know, monastics. Any persons drawn to Jesus in the first third of the first century would have been peasants at the margins of poverty or even over the edge into what John Dominic Crossan calls "destitution."

So they were very much in and *of* the world, though their world was a first-century combination of contemporary Bosnia and Calcutta: harsh, uncaring and terminally deprived.

The key to understanding what the phrase "not of this world" means is the word "world" itself. It is the Greek "cosmos," which means "the orderly, harmonious, systematic universe." Our word "cosmopolitan" derives from "cosmos." It is an adjective used to describe sophistication, affluence, social acceptance and broad significance.

As we know from our study of first-century Palestine, though, those who were drawn to John the Baptist and to Jesus were people largely out of the economic and social mainstream, marginalized by economics, social and political policies and programs enforced by a militaristic oligarchy of the dominant Roman government of occupation.

Of that world, the Jesus people surely were not. There was

not much order, harmony or system about their lives — especially the homeless wanderers among them. Luke and other first-century writers are careful to portray Jesus in solidarity with the poor and destitute — on the side of the have-nots and against the haves.

How, then, has the church strayed so far from that original center? And why? The answer to "how" is that the earthy, revolutionary wisdom of Jesus that had to do with economic and social justice got caught up in the years after his death with other not always compatible agenda, as later Christian writers attempted for all kinds of reasons to turn the bare-bones story of a Palestinian peasant revolutionary into a myth of epic proportion.

In that myth, Jesus became a king and a lord, and inevitably a retinue of hierarchs emerged as a kind of royal court as the church adopted the military discipline system of its worst enemy — the Roman army — as its order. (The word "diocese" means "military district" as in a jurisdiction ruled under martial law.) That's the "how?"

Here's the "why?" Jesus' revolutionary commentary and teachings gained such a wide following among Palestinian peasantry that, as depicted in the gospels, the ruling authorities found it necessary to silence Jesus. But evidently they could not silence his message by silencing him. So the message continued to be transmitted.

Some number of Jews in the first century who were not poor and not destitute and therefore with social and economic interests to protect took over the message of Jesus, softened it and adapted it so that it became less offensive. It was no longer "a stone to make people stumble and a rock that made them fall."

Later the Emperor Constantine finished the job by declaring that Christianity was to be the sole officially sanctioned religion of the Roman Empire, thus rendering the church innocuous except as the emperor might deploy its resources. And knowing about emperors — especially Roman ones — you would not expect much of a benign use of such resources.

Where are we today with all this? Where the contemporary Roman Catholic Church has attempted to side with the poor, especially in Central and Latin America, the Vatican has sharply curtailed its priests and bishops.

The church, in fact, is not on the side of the economically and socially marginalized in very effective ways. Why not? If the people Jesus cared about in the first century and about whom we as Jesus people should likewise be caring about in the 20th century do not "belong to this world," why not?

If the homeless, if the urban and rural poor do not have a consistent part in the orderly, harmonious and systematic cosmos, don't blame it on them. Don't blame it on God. God has shown us in the teachings and examples of Jesus what to do. We have the power to do it. Why don't we, doesn't the church, doesn't Christianity, do it?

JOHN 17:1-11

The bumper sticker on the car ahead of mine — both stopped dead in an interminable traffic jam — read "PRAYER CHANGES THINGS." I was certain that somewhere in that impatient welter of trembling steel and rubber there were expostulations being uttered involving words like "god" and "Christ," and for all I knew some of them may have been actually parts of prayers. If so, prayer did not change the gridlock. But one man pulled his car to the shoulder, got out and began intelligently and authoritatively to direct traffic and, in due course, we were all on our way. I thought then that a more accurate rendition of the bumper sticker might be "PEOPLE CHANGE THINGS." An approaching thunderstorm caught my eye as the sun faded behind massive clouds, and I thought that things, like the weather, often just change themselves.

To whom is Jesus talking in the prayer that appears in this

gospel reading? John, no doubt, would have the reader believe that it is God. It is also John who created the image of Jesus as logos being one with God (John 1:2). John 1:2 and 17 taken together put the concept of prayer in a new light because at some level prayer is talking to oneself ... meaning that the responsibility to change things (or to deal intelligently with things that are beyond our power to change) rests with us. It seems reasonable to believe that the natural order produces results that are to a greater or lesser degree predictable: floods, climatic conditions, human behavior that issues in violence and destruction. Asking God to make those things go away seems irrational and beside the point. Not deforesting the land, not polluting the air and water supplies and dedicating political capital to the easing of economic injustice would seem the rational things to do.

Similarly, it is an abdication of our responsibility to pray for peace without working for it, to pray for health without working to improve or maintain it, to pray for strength without summoning up that which is in us already, to pray for others without reaching out to them in effective ways.

LUKE 1:39-49

The New Testament scholar John Dominic Crossan has reminded us of the political and economic conditions to which Palestinian peasants were subjected in the first third of the first century C.E. The lucky were merely poor; the unfortunate were destitute. It was therefore natural that leaders and movements of opposition arose. They were generally of two kinds: apocalyptic and wisdom-oriented. The zealots, the assassins (siccaroi) and individuals like John the Baptist were among the first. Jesus of Nazareth was among the second. The first kind had basically written off the world as it was and resorted to terrorism and violence because there was nothing to lose, or, as in the Baptist's case, as a call to repent and get ready for imminent judgment. John may have preached apocalypticism, but there is no evidence that he was a kinetic extremist. The second kind, including Jesus, appeared to have believed that the world was potentially an OK place if only people would do to others as they would have done to themselves, etc., etc., etc. For the first type the "rule of God" was to be hoped for as a judgmental intervention of God; for the second, the "rule of God" was at hand and depended only on human beings to embrace it through the living out of basic ethical principles.

Both John and Jesus were Jews — Jesus certainly of the peasant class because he came from the distinctly peasant village of Nazareth. John's background is less certain, though there was something about his presentation of himself that suggests he may have had some connection with the semi-monastic Essenes. Either way, both came on the public scene in that time of tension and conflict, and both seemed to be partisans of the economically oppressed. It is unclear from conflicting accounts if the one knew the other or even that the other existed. But two prominent gospel stories were written to connect them. The first is the story of Jesus' baptism by John, otherwise an odd tale since it is doubtful that Jesus would have identified with John's apocalypticism. Jesus was from Galilee; John from Judea. John differed from Jesus in approach as shouting from a fire escape differs from gentle discourse.

The second story that links them is the one before us from Luke's hand. It is the improbable story that links them as blood relatives through their mothers. There is no evidence at all that this story is a) a historical account or b) that it was meant to be taken as such. Luke is the supreme storyteller. His nativity narrative, charming and memorable though it is, is pointedly a fiction. So the question to ask is: "What profound truth was Luke wanting to convey in this story?" Some interpreters see Luke's gospel as essentially humanitarian in nature, so he might have been trying to consolidate all the forces, however compatible, that were for economic and social justice (see Luke 1:51-53, also I Samuel 2:1-10).

The gospel is otherwise filled with compassion and so humanistic in its approach, so attuned to human suffering and its relief. From Luke's late first-century C.E. perspective, why would he not have seen the teacher of ethical wisdom from Galilee and the brash reformer from Judea as two sides of the same coin, as bearing witness to the same divine thirst for justice? So typical of his poetic creativity, he crafted the truly beautiful story of Mary and Elizabeth, forever tying their sons together.

ACTS 2:1-11

The dramatic account of the descent of the holy spirit upon the apostolic community is by no means an eyewitness account. It is an introductory story in the second of two lengthy narratives attributed by tradition to Luke and were composed about 50-60 years after the time in which Jesus would have lived. We can assume that this story grew out of what must have been a troublesome problem those of early Christianity experienced as they struggled to connect their beliefs and practices — by then considerably different from those of their original Judaism — with Jesus long since gone. The concept of a spiritual presence of Jesus among members of those communities must have gone a considerable distance toward solving that problem. Luke, as with the angelic chorus in the nativity narrative, employed the flamboyant as he wrote of mighty gusts of wind, eerie tongues of flame and people speaking in a babble of languages. That imagery doesn't quite work now. So we may turn to John who saw the spiritual presence in a more nuanced, subtle way.

In John 20:19-23, the spirit is conferred in the breathing of a not-quite-corporeal Jesus upon the disciples — reminiscent of the breath of Elohim upon the face of the deep (Genesis 1:2). The next words are monumentally significant to understanding where John was going with this: "Receive the Holy Spirit; whose sins you forgive, they are forgiven." John is saying that the spirit of Jesus will be knowable in a culture of forgiveness, when and where people are able and willing to let go resentments and grudges, to give up claims for revenge and satisfaction when they can and do forgive those who trespass against them.

MATTHEW 28:16-20

The so-called Great Commission to convert the world to Jesus has often been taken as divine license to do just that with spectacularly bad results. The Crusades come to mind, as well as the latter-day 1996 resolve of the Southern Baptist Convention to convert American Jews. Religion is clearly a free-market enterprise, and it stands to reason that you have every right to try to sell me your religion and vice versa. Sales is one thing. Overt coercion is another. Meanwhile, imagine how old Sam Goldwyn would have portrayed the scene of The Great Commission: the resurrected Jesus being worshiped on a mountaintop by adoring disciples and Jesus with an expansive, triumphalist gesture commissioning them to conquer the world in his name. The accompanying music would need to be of the "Star Wars" quality with wraparound Dolby sound that would rattle your innards. Goldwyn would probably gloss right over the qualification Matthew felt obligated to include in his otherwise perfect story: the phrase, "But some doubted." The word doubt here is the Greek *distadzo* which can mean "to hesitate." Might the phrase be better translated as, "But there was some hesitation"?

Why would there be hesitation on the part of those who are said by Matthew to have witnessed in person the resurrected Jesus? What more need be known? Matthew must have known what we know, i.e., that neither doubt nor hesitancy is a sin. If, indeed, the human being has evolved with reasoning powers, it must mean that we are not meant blindly to accept dogma but to examine and question what we are asked to accept and to require of it that it be rational. Matthew portrays 11 men who are standing in the presence of one who was dead and is evidently alive again. And they are experiencing, some of them, hesitancy as to whether what they're seeing is really there and if they dare to base the rest of their lives on the possibility of its being real.

That, of course, is the fault line on which aspiring Christians have ever stood. The one proclaimed as risen is the one who taught people to sell all they have and give the proceeds to the poor, to turn the other cheek, to walk the second mile and all that other wisdom we know but often fail to act out. Except, as Matthew observed, there was some hesitation — and there still is. I think that means that you and I — all that space and time away from whatever it was that transpired in the first century C.E. — will always be hesitant in commitment, will always be taking one step forward and two back, will always be one day sure and the next uncertain. And I think that is all right. As a very wise person once told me: "It's OK to be where you are as long as you know you don't have to stay there."

MATTHEW 11:25-30

What occurs in this passage is an abrupt softening of what up to now in the flow of Matthew's prose has been a hard message. First we heard Jesus sending out his disciples as sheep into the jaws of wolves, into an environment in which brother will betray brother to death and where all who teach and live Jesus' way will be hated by all. In the very next passage: "Do not think that I have come to bring peace to earth, but a sword ... those who find their lives will lose them, etc., etc." The final words of this passage? "Take my yoke upon you ... for my yoke is easy and my burden is light."

What we're seeing in this progression is history unfolding. The earlier passages represented the first enthusiasm of a new movement brash in its recruitment strategy. It was flush with the realization that Rome, with all its dread power, inexplicably had not succeeded in eradicating what had begun with Jesus' ethical and wisdom teaching. Soon enough, though, persecution and other difficulties began to take their toll. As the ranks of the committed were thinned, as it grew more difficult to espouse the cause, the church changed its strategy. Now the yoke would be easy and the burden light.

This is not to say that it was a calculated change in strategy. At some point in any lived-out commitment that puts one at odds with the majority, one reaches what the marathon runner calls "the wall." And once one passes through that wall a kind of euphoria sets in. In my jogging days, I set a goal of being able to run around a park in the Detroit River known as Belle Isle. The course was 7.2 miles long. It took about a year to get my middle-aged body ready for that test. But the day came, and off I set. After the first third of the distance, I was glad I had undertaken the test. I felt good, optimistic and I bore down and ran faster. As I entered the final third of the way, I began to doubt that I would make it alive. And then with less than a mile to go, I passed through the wall and fairly coasted into the goal with a smile on my face and pain a distant runner-up.

What the wall and the euphoria signify is that one who has gone the distance and suffered the pain has learned not only endurance but that one can endure. The yoke, in the end, is easy because it has been borne. The burden, in the end, is light because it has been carried. That is why the casual Christian will never get over the annoyance the demands of commitment make. To the non-runner or occasional walker, 7.2 miles' worth of jogging seems impossible. To the dabbler, religious commitment, in this case to the living out of Jesus' ethical principles, is both unattainable and undoable.

MATTHEW 14:22-33

The college football coach stood threateningly over the freshmen recruits on a hot muggy August morning. "OK, dogs," he growled, "I know some of you guys think you can walk on water. I just want to see if any of you can swim." He meant, of course, that miracles didn't win football games, only discipline and hard work. I suppose the coach's remark was a veiled reference to the episode of Jesus walking on water and Peter's flailing Australian crawl — a story that is important for us and the religious movement of which we are a part in the rough seas of a postmodern world. It is a world out of which basic humanitarian values and respect seem to have flown so that those who would maintain and cultivate them are rather like the disciples' little boat foundering in the waves. That is the sense of the story Matthew appropriated from Mark and edited to suit his own late first-century purposes.

By the time Matthew got into the business of church leadership in Syria, ca. 75-85 C.E., the church's mission was taking shape. It was seeking recruits from among Gentiles. And its job was made the more difficult because its putative leader had not been on the scene for 50 years. That reality is represented by the transition from the passage that precedes this one. The so-called "feeding of the 5,000" has been accomplished when Matthew narrates: "Immediately Jesus made the disciples get into the boat and go on ahead." And that was the way it was by Matthew's time. The leaders of the movement, such as they may have been, were "on ahead" and by themselves in the vortex of events encountering heavy weather and a rough go.

We are told that Jesus overtook the disciples' storm-tossed craft by walking on the sea. But because human beings do not walk on water, the disciples are said to have panicked. What they saw was an apparition. Yet Peter, as his character is here manipulated by Matthew, takes the chance that it might actually be Jesus and so calls out. He is invited to step out of the boat and join Jesus on the rolling swells.

The all-too-glib Western take on this is that Jesus was defying physics. But the first-century Hebraic mind would see in that picture the creative force astride the primordial chaos represented, as it was commonly, by the sea whence came all life. Jesus' invitation to Peter is Matthew saying to his fellow Christians that their mission was not to traverse chaos in a leaky boat but to leap into the chaos at hand and help wrest order from it.

This is, of course, a call to the contemporary church to take itself out of its antiseptic cloister and get into the mix of real life, to apply in effective action the ethical principles of Jesus, thus to bring some order out of the social chaos that marks our time.

A Personal Word

The impulse that became this book I probably felt first in June 1949, when I was a pupil in a vacation bible school put on by a Methodist Church in the small northern Michigan village in which I grew up. Our family was generally a churchgoing family, and I grew up hearing the old Protestant hymns, learning memory verses from the bible and with that general view of things that Sunday schools of the era tended to suggest, viz., that God saw all, knew all and that you had better behave. Why more of us didn't always behave was a curiosity to me, and I remember engaging my father, now of blessed memory, in several searching conversations about why, if when in Sunday school I believed God was watching my every move, at other times I did and said things of which the God of my Sunday school would surely disapprove. Since no one close to me had yet died and because life for our family was the typically task-oriented, goal-seeking life of the postwar years, the subject of "heaven" and the possible desirability of going there never came up.

That summer, though, of 1949 a new and alien force entered

the social complex of the village in the person of a young woman schoolteacher with boundless energy and a tent-evangelist's fervor. She was the first fundamentalist Christian, but, alas, not the last I would know. She virtually took over the Sunday school of the one church in town and, to the delight of the minister, filled it up. She could play ball with the most athletic of the boys and beat anyone in a foot race. She sang like a nightingale and told stories, biblical and otherwise, that made you sit on the edge of your seat. Besides everything else, she was physically a knockout. It goes without saying that I fell for her hook, line and sinker and she soon owned me lock, stock and barrel.

It was from her lips during vacation bible school that I first heard the popular and dread concepts of heaven and hell in the most vivid and frightening terms. Heaven is where you got to go when you died, provided that you had been "saved." Hell with its unbelievable and unbearable yet unending torment is where you went if you weren't. To my horror I learned that it was not in the final analysis my misdeeds that would bar me from heaven — Jesus had already died for my sins. What would bar me from heaven and be a one-way ticket to hell was my inability or unwillingness to believe that certain things were so, including that Jesus had to bleed on the cross because God demanded human blood as payment for human sins and that Jesus could take my sin away because he was God's son. I also would have to believe that he was physically raised from the dead and that he had been born of a human mother but sired by a spirit rather than a man.

To a 10-year-old boy who to date had been reared on a fairly rational basis, this was psychic overload. I knew that I could not control my doubt about some things. And I knew that if I *said* I believed but really didn't I would be in even worse trouble with God. My dream life descended into the nightmarish as prepuberty sexual fantasies involving the aforementioned Sunday school teacher freely mixed with horrendous images of hell fire and punishment. Fifty years later I would have been taken to a psychiatrist. But in rural northern Michigan in 1949, I was on my own.

Complicating all this was my affinity with the rituals of the church and its music. Methodists can really sing, and when the choir included a redheaded girl on whom, in addition to the teacher and for different reasons, I had the biggest of crushes, the singing filled me with wondrous emotion and the rituals with a mindless kind of pride at belonging to something that seemed to make me special. And so on I marched into adolescence burdened by a kind of intellectual schizophrenia, loving the outward realities of the church's life all mixed up with the sin of loving two females at a time — one of them more than twice my age! My terrible secret was that I did not and could not believe in much of the content — but I was trying mightily.

Then came along a new experience — church camp. Off I went with others, one being the redheaded girl from the choir, to Camp Lake Louise, a collection of lodges and cabins on the wooded shores of a pristine inland lake. For a week the camp pulsed with the hormones of a hundred adolescent boys and girls, the mesmerizing four-part harmony on such hymns as "Let the lower lights be burning," "Fairest Lord Jesus," and "O for a closer walk with God," and the enthralling camp fires as ministers milked bible stories for all they were worth in an effort to give at least 100 convinced Christian youths to a world that surely needed them. Yet, still in some zone of my consciousness I felt like an intruder. There I was singing my heart out and eating my heart out at the same time. Then shortly after I returned home from camp my mother died from stomach cancer at the age of 36. That brought heaven directly into the picture.

Our minister spent a lot of time with my father, my two sisters and me in the hours and days following mother's death. And what he had to say only deepened my anxiety. He told us that God must have wanted my mother "to come home to Him," that He needed her more than we did and that perhaps the weeks of agony that preceded her death were a test of her and of us. In any event, the minister said, it had to be God's will, and we should find comfort in that.

For a long time after that — even as I continued to participate in the church's ritual life and youth fellowship — I hated God for what our minister said His will was, and I doubted very much that my mother was anywhere but in her grave in the local cemetery. Thus did the gulf between outward observance and inward belief deepen. I couldn't believe, yet I could not bear to leave what I had come to love. For a lot longer than other people had any hint of, I considered studying to become a minister even though by high school I said I wanted to be a journalist. Years later I came to understand why journalism became a substitute for the ministry: In journalism you simply found out the facts and wrote them up. Belief in stuff you couldn't see, and that you deemed irrational, never came into the picture. In the long term, ministry won out because I couldn't live without the music and ritual and the emotional lift it gave me and the sense of belonging it afforded. Except for seven years of doing both professional ministry and journalism and eight more solely working for a newspaper, my adult life has otherwise been given to the ministry.

A long and difficult pilgrimage has ensued these 30-plus years, as in sermons, lectures and teaching catechism, I have parsed and pared scripture and doctrine in ways that I could live with intellectually. That has gotten me into trouble with three different congregations but also won approbation from many among them. Along the way, I have repeatedly tested a hypothesis and privately elevated it to a theory, namely that in every congregation three general groups exist. The first is a small but vocal minority of people who range from utter fundamentalism to brittle traditionalism, for whom no point of faith is unresolved and ambiguity is unknown. A fit motto for that kind would be this legend I once saw on a banner at a church convention: "GOD SAID IT! I BELIEVE IT! AND THAT'S THAT!" Ah, what a comfortable world.

The second and by far the largest grouping includes those upon whom doctrine and scriptural interpretation are largely lost so long as the minister is nice, the music decent and the fellowship congenial. To members of this group, heterodoxy and orthodoxy are six of one and a half dozen of the other, and in saying this I do not mean to make a slur on their intellects. For one reason or another, they choose not to care. The third group, again small but hardly ever vocal are the seekers, the creative doubters, the keen observers and clear thinkers who welcome challenge; indeed they invite it. They want to be some place other than where received tradition has brought them. In my experience, these are the people who, if encouraged by the minister and not terminally discouraged by the militant fundamentalist-traditionalists, will enliven a congregation and make it a fun place to be. This third group will not last long, much less flourish, if the ministerial leadership is static, unadventurous and threatened by the fundamentalist-traditionalists.

It is to this third group or type that I have always beamed my message, for whom I have prepared sermons and lectures, because in such people I believe the future relevancy of Christianity rests. Without them, the faith is doomed to end up with all the creativity and effectiveness of a secret lodge with strange costumes, empty ritual and no substance. Resistance to exploration, change and transformation will only abet the already growing irrelevance of much of Christianity. Its myths are useful only if they are acknowledged as such, and its proclamations valid if they are acknowledged as provisional and contingent.

This book is an effort to persuade church leaders, both lay and clergy, to lay aside alien worldviews and the traditions that have sprung from them and to claim the freedom that reason brings to those who rely on it. For churches and their constituent congregations to expend capital on defending the indefensible is to invite eventual bankruptcy. In this regard, it will be important for a rationally based Christianity to grow up where human sexuality is concerned and to quickly and persuasively argue that homosexuality is part of the spectrum of all sexuality and in no way intrinsically evil any more than heterosexuality is evil. It is, of course, how people act out whatever their sexuality is that counts — whether responsibly and faithfully or in ways that compromise others. The current preoccupation with homosexuality that has several mainline Protestant denominations in its grip must cease. Someone — several someones in each denomination — must say and say loudly that one or two ancient prohibitions of homosexual conduct cannot rationally be construed as meaning God is against it and, furthermore, that what most competent persons in the psychiatric community have long since concluded, viz., that homosexuality is only a statistical abnormality, is the reasonable position.

A rationally based Christianity needs to seize the issues of contraception and euthanasia out of the grasping hands of the male-dominated and misogynist Roman Catholic hierarchy and the Christian right and from their fundamentalist, self-serving interpretations of them. Contraception and euthanasia are two of the most freeing gifts humanity has ever given itself. The liberty to enjoy the profound and fulfilling pleasures of sexuality without the concern of bringing children into the world has freed women as nothing else has. To proscribe contraception is the height of unreason and mental cruelty. Moreover, reproductive rights, including abortion when deemed necessary by a woman and her physician, are part of that freedom. Euthanasia — and not necessarily the bizarre sort that Jack Kevorkian trades in — is likewise a freedom that we have bestowed on ourselves. If a person can state rationally that because of whatever pain and suffering he or she may be enduring he or she wants to end life, why should that option be denied him or her? Certainly by no absolutist injunction handed down by a hierarchy or tribunal which says it represents the will of an unseen god. Whenever religious authority appeals to the absolute and unambiguous will of a god neither you nor they can see or know by any process of reason, beware.

A religion that had its inception in the ethical and wisdom teachings of an obscure Galilean peasant who did not trade or converse in absolutist or triumphalist terms must seek to recover a sense of its origins. The original Jesus appears to have spoken with irony, ambiguity and sometimes puzzling humor. His sayings invite consideration, examination and trying on for size.

A post-credal church, a Christianity beyond creeds, will seek a life that reflects the profound simplicity of those sayings, their avoidance of bombast and conceit. A post-credal church will be a seeking, searching church that embraces ambiguity and is content to speak provisionally about what it thinks may be true in a given time and place. It will be like Willa Cather's archbishop: unwilling to accept patently absurd interpretations of observable phenomena, and finally unwilling to build its intellectual house on the sands of unreason.

Appendix A:
Unpacking Resurrection-Speak

As recently as the mid-1960s, no less a theologian than Jurgen Moltmann said, "Christianity stands or falls with the reality of the raising of Jesus from the dead by God" (*The Theology of Hope*, 1967). This cannot be so unless Moltmann does not mean actual physical resurrection on that particular "third day." Nothing in the New Testament gives an actual description of the resurrection, rather what is reported is what people said they experienced, or, more accurately, what other people said other people experienced. No one who is said to have spoken of the resurrection said he or she was an eyewitness.

The closest, perhaps, to any so-called description of the "event" can be found in the Gospel of Peter 9:35-40, thus: "Now in the night in which the Lord's day dawned, when the soldiers, two by two in every watch, were keeping guard, there rang out a loud voice in heaven, and they saw the heavens opened and two men came down from there in a great brightness and draw nigh to the sepulchre. That stone which had been laid against the entrance to the sepulchre started of itself to roll and gave way to the side, and the sepulchre was opened, and both the young men entered in. When now the soldiers saw this, they awakened the centurion and the elders. ... And whilst they were relating what they had seen, they saw again three men come out from the sepulchre, and two of them sustaining the other, and a cross following them, and the heads of the two reaching to heaven, but that of him who was led of them by the hand overpassing the heavens." (The most accessible source for the Gospel of Peter and other non-canonical texts may be the paperback *The Other Gospels*, edited by Ron Cameron, 1982, Westminster Press-Philadelphia, in which the above passage appears at page 80.)

Aside from the obvious clues that what is "described" here is a vision is the fact that the first known use of the Gospel of Peter was in Syria around 200 C.E., suggesting it may have been composed well after the canonical gospels. So compelling is the "vision," though, that one supposes the framers of the canon, had they known of it, might have included or integrated it or at least appended it in some way to the synoptics and/or John.

The earliest New Testament mention of the resurrection occurs in Paul's correspondence with the Corinthian communities (I. 15:1-11). Paul speaks in this letter around 50 A.D. of a tradition he received. Received whence or from whom? Certainly not from the Quelle sayings or from the Gospel of Thomas, the writing of which would possibly have been contemporary with Paul. (Thomas has no passion/resurrection narrative.) Was the mythmaking already in process by 50 A.D., that is the turning of fragments of a largely lost life of Jesus into a full-blown myth of the Christ? Possibly. And Paul, not unfamiliar with the Hellenistic culture in which he moved and which was rife with myth, might have begun it himself. It has been noted above how some passages of his correspondence to various Christian communities have the flavor of myth about them. Yet Paul never deals with the details of the resurrection, though he claims to have been in the presence of a risen one (I Corinthians 15:8). He seems simply to take Jesus' resurrection as axiomatic and moves on from there.

In fact, nothing in the New Testament canon offers — as one might expect if it actually physically occurred and could in some way be corroborated by independent and/or authoritative sources — a clear account of the event itself, only contradictory accounts of what people said happened to them in the aftermath of Jesus' death. This suggests that all the "resurrection talk" found in the New Testament is the product of human industry, all the way from wishful thinking to hallucination. It is often said that "something" must have happened to have made the apostolic community and its successors so bold and brave against the foes that would crush the movement. Ignatius of Antioch's letter *To the Romans*, Chapter 5, pleads with Christians there not to take any steps to save him from martyrdom: "May I have the joy of the beasts that are prepared for me ... that I may attain unto Jesus Christ." Some 40 years later in 156 C.E., a purported witness to the martyrdom of Polycarp of Smyrna quotes the venerable bishop, in the moments before the kindling of the pyre that would consume him, as saying, "I bless thee in that thou hast deemed me worthy of this hour ... for this cause ... I praise thee" (*Apostolic Fathers* XIV. 2-3).

In both cases, martyrdom was a foregone conclusion, unless either had recanted. But life unmasked as craven pretenders would have been unthinkable for either Ignatius or Polycarp. No less so for Hugh Latimer and his fellow Anglican martyr Nicolas Ridley. As the faggots at their feet were lighted, Latimer was heard to cry out: "Be of good comfort, Master Ridley, and play the man; we shall this day light such a candle by God's grace in England as I trust shall never be put out" (*Acts and Monuments*, J. Foxe, ed. J. Pratt, 1877, Vol. VII, p. 550). Would it not have been principle and dignity which moved all such to stand firm even in the face of death?

Meanwhile, just a cursory examination of several texts in the canonical gospels — all of which were written no fewer than 35-40 years after the time Jesus would have been resurrected — clearly show, the disciples and their associates in unheroic postures. And the gospels were written against the backdrop of the supposed resurrection! See: Matthew 8:24-25, 14:25-26, 15:21-23, 16:21-22, 26:31-35 (compare 69-75), 28:17b; Mark 6:47-50, 8:31-33, 9:17-18, 30-32, 38-39, 10:35-40, 14:66-72, 16:8; Luke 8:22-24, 9:33- 46, 18:31-34, 22:24, 31-34 (compare to 22:54-62); John 6:16-19, 60-61, 18:15-27, 20:24-25.

And examine for yourself in detail the passion narratives and ask yourself which of the disciples (other than John in *John*) is depicted as being present or doing more than Peter in lopping off the ears of the high priest's slave (John 18:10). It remained for Luke to make the disciples — Peter and John in particular, then later Barnabas and Paul — into heroes in the Acts of the Apostles. But if they had been such when the supposedly original "push" became "shove," why did no one report it, and why did the evangelists who wrote against the backdrop of their resurrection stories not say so?

The time has come to say that, even with the bible in hand, belief in the physical resurrection of Jesus is unsupportable. It is not a fact of history but a projection of, at the best, faith and, at the worst, delusion. And to say that is not, as some would retort, to pull the underpinnings from Christianity. Christianity that is to be relevant and useful in the real world will be the celebration and living out of the ethical principles and fundamental wisdom teachings of Jesus, whoever he was, whenever and wherever he was born and however he died.

Whether he died by crucifixion and his body was left to rot and be consumed by vultures and/or dogs (as was the charming Roman custom), or whether illness, accident or old age overtook him and his body was buried, the stuff that was his body has long since rejoined the chemical and molecular structure of earth.

If 21st-century Christians will give all their religious energy to the living out of Jesus' deceptively simple principles, a revolution may occur that might raise him from the grave in which he and his principles have long since been buried. That would make the physical resurrection look like a cheap trick.

Appendix B:
What Jesus May Have Actually Said

B
ecause of repeated references to the ethical and wisdom teaching of Jesus in the main body of this book, it seemed important to reprint what the author (backed up by much of the non-ideological community of New Testament scholarship) believes constitutes that teaching. Based on the theory that Jesus was an itinerant sage or street speaker, that he did not proclaim himself as anything other than what he was, that he was not an apocalyptic preacher looking for the end of the world, that he did not aggressively seek out verbal confrontation, that he spoke minimally but pithily and that a whole religious institution was founded around him and his teaching by persons not embarrassed by greatly embellishing his character and therefore his supposed sayings, what follows here is a gospel by gospel listing of what Jesus may reasonably be believed to have said. Of course, oral tradition by which surely many, if not all, of these sayings were first transmitted has its obvious problems with accuracy.

The criteria for including a passage among sayings of Jesus

thought to be authentic (if not preserved verbatim) is that each appeared in the Quelle corpus, the Gospel of Thomas or in Mark. Where a saying is repeated by Matthew or appropriated and revised by him, notation is made. Where a saying appears only in Matthew or Luke and not in the Quelle, Mark or Thomas and appears in what follows here, the criterion for inclusion is that the saying sounds very much like something the Jesus of the other sayings included would have said. Similar sayings or stories that appear in Luke — but nowhere else — are excluded from this grouping because of Luke's apparent remoteness from the Palestinian traditions and because it is clear that Luke was a novelist at heart.

In some cases, the New Revised Standard Version translation has been used, but many sources were consulted, including the author's own translation and/or paraphrase.

MARK

2:17 The well have no need of a physician, but the ill do.

2:19 The groom's friends can't fast while the groom is present, can they? So long as the groom is around, you can't expect them to fast. (Thomas 104)

2:22a No one (who knows what he's doing) puts new wine into old skins because the wine will burst the old skins (because they are shrunken and dried out). (also Thomas 47)

2:27 The sabbath was created for the sake of people, not people for the sake of the sabbath.

3:27 No one can break into a powerful person's house and take his belongings until he binds that person; then the house can be looted. (Thomas 35 and Quelle)

4:3-8 Hear this! A sower went out to sow. As he sowed some seed fell on the path and the birds alit and ate it up. Some (of the seed) fell on rocky ground on which was not much soil, and it sprouted quickly because the soil had no depth. So when the sun rose, the young wheat was scorched, and as it had no roots (to speak of), it withered. Other of the seed fell among (a certain kind of weed that grows quickly and spreads), and the wheat was overcome and did not bear grain. But some of the seed fell on good ground where it came up and produced grain, (and the yield was tremendous). (Thomas 9)

4:21 Why would one bring a lamp only to put it under a bushel basket or under the bed rather than on a lamp stand? (Thomas 33 and Quelle)

4:25 For to those who have more, more will be given; and from those who have nothing, it, too, will be taken away. (Thomas 41 and Quelle)

4:26 The rule of God is like this: a person scatters seed on the ground and goes to sleep at night and gets up in the morning — all the while the seed sprouts and grows, and he hasn't any idea of how. The ground produces this crop by itself: first the stalk, then the ear, then the full grain in the ear. But when the crop is ready (the farmer) goes at it with the sickle because it is time for the harvest (to begin). (Thomas 21)

4:30 How does one describe this "rule of God"? Or what parable can be used (to account for it?) It is like the mustard seed, which, when it is sown, is the smallest of seeds ... but when it comes up it becomes taller than most shrubs with such large branches that birds make nests in its shade. (Thomas 20 and Quelle)

6:4 A prophet is respected except in the town he is from and among his relatives and at home. (Thomas 31)

7:14b-15 Listen to me, all of you, and (try to) understand: It is not what goes into a person from outside that defiles him; but what comes out of him — that's what defiles. (Thomas 14)

9:50 Salt is good, unless it loses its flavor. Then how do you restore it? (Quelle)

10:14b Let these children come right up to me. Don't even try to stop them because the Rule of God belongs to them (as they are).

10:23 How very difficult it is for those who are well off to be a part of God's rule.

10:25 It is easier for that camel over there to get itself through the eye of a needle than for the well-off to feel at home under the reign of God.

10:31 Many who are first (now) will end up being last, and those who are last (now) will end up being first. (Thomas 4)

12:17 Give to Caesar the things that are (obviously) Caesar's, and to God what are God's. (Thomas 100) (See also Romans 12:17.)

12:38-39 Beware the scribes. They like to walk around in long robes and to be greeted with deference in the marketplaces and to have the best seats in the synagogues and places of honor at dinner parties. These are the ones who appropriate widow's homes and for the sake of appearances say long prayers. But they won't get away with it. (Quelle)

MATTHEW

5:3 Happy like the gods are the poor in spirit for the reign of Heaven belongs to them. (Thomas 54 and Quelle)

5:4 Happy like the gods are those who are grieving, for they will be consoled. (Quelle)

5:6 Happy like the gods are those who are hungry and thirsty for justice, they will eat and drink their fill. (Thomas 69 and Quelle)

5:10 Happy like the gods are you when people vilify you, persecute you and falsely charge you with evil because of your connection with me (and my words). (Remember that) this is the way they persecuted the prophets before you (and me). (Thomas 69 and Quelle)

5:13 (see Mark 9:50 above)

5:14 (see Mark 4:21 above)

5:25-26 Come to terms quickly with one who accuses you while on the way (to court) with him or else the accuser may hand you over to the judge to the guard and you will be thrown into prison. I tell you, you'll never get out until you have paid the last cent (of your fine). (Quelle)

5:39-42 Don't resist one who is evil. But if anyone strikes you on the right cheek, turn the other to him as well. And if one wants to sue you for your coat, give up your cloak as well. If (a Roman solider) presses you into (carrying his gear) one mile (which is his right), go a second mile (voluntarily). Give to any who ask. (Thomas 95 and Quelle)

5:44-45 Love your enemies ... for (God) makes the sun to rise on the evil and the good, and sends rain on the just and the unjust. If you love those who love you, what is the point? Even tax collectors do the same. (Quelle)

6:3 When you give alms, do not let your left hand know what your right hand is doing. (Thomas 62)

6:6, 9, 10a, 11-12, 14-15 When you pray, go into your rooms and shut the door ... and pray like this: Our Father, your name be revered. Let your rule be the only one. Give us what we need today, and release us from what we owe to the degree we release those who owe us. ... For if you forgive others their failures and offenses, your heavenly Father will also forgive you. But if you don't forgive them, your Father won't forgive yours. (Thomas 14 and Quelle)

6:24 No one can be the slave of two (different) owners because he will either dislike the first and prefer the second or be loyal to the first and hate the second. You cannot be a slave to God and money (at the same time). (Thomas 47 and Quelle)

6:25-31 So, I tell you, do not worry about your life, that is what you will eat or what you will drink, or about your body, what you will wear. Is not life more than food, and the body more than clothing? Consider the birds in the air; they neither sow nor reap or store food away, yet your heavenly Father feeds them. Aren't you worth more than they are? Can you by worrying about things like that add anything to yourself or lengthen your life? And why worry about clothing? Look at the lilies of the field, how it is that they grow; they neither toil nor spin. Yet even Solomon in all his glory was not arrayed like one of them. But if God so dresses up the weeds in the field which grow today and tomorrow are tossed into an oven, will he not with greater care clothe you few of faith? So do not be concerned, saying "What will I eat, or what will I drink or what will I wear?" (Thomas 36 and Quelle)

7:3-5 Why look at the splinter in your brother's eye but fail to notice the log in your own? How can you say, "Let me take the splinter out of your eye," when all the while that log is in your own? You actor! First take the log out of your own eye, then you'll be able to see clearly enough to remove the splinter from your brother's eye. (Thomas 26 and Quelle)

7:7-8 Ask, and it will be given to you, seek and you will find, knock and the door will be opened for you. (Thomas 2, 92, 94 and Quelle)

7:12 Treat other people the way you want them to treat you. (Thomas 6 & Quelle)

7:13 Go in by the narrow gate, for the wide gate and the easy way lead to destruction. The gate is narrow and the way hard that leads to life, and few find and use it. (Quelle)

7:16b You will know people by what they produce. Are grapes gathered from thorns or figs from thistles? (Thomas 45 and Quelle)

8:22b Follow me, and leave the dead to bury their dead. (Quelle)

9:12b, 13b (see Mark 2:17)

9:15a (see Mark 2:22a)

9:16-17 (see Mark 2:22a & Thomas 47)

10:16b You must be as astute as serpents and guileless as doves. (Thomas 39)

11:7b-8 What did you think you would see in the desert? A reed shaking in the wind? What *did* you go out there to see? One clad in expensive clothing? Never mind. Those who wear expensive clothes live in palaces. (Thomas 78 and Quelle)

12:11-12 Suppose one of you has a single sheep and it falls into a deep hole on sabbath, would you not do all you could to get it out? So certainly it is all right to do a good thing on sabbath. (Mark 3:1-6)

12:29 (see Mark 3:27 & Quelle)

13:3b-8 (see Mark 4:3-8) (Thomas 9)

13:12 (see Mark 4:25) (Thomas 41)

13:31b-32 (see Mark 4:30) (Thomas 20 and Quelle)

13:33b The rule of Heaven is like leaven that a woman took and hid in 50 pounds of flour until the whole business was leavened. (Thomas 96 and Quelle)

13:44-46 The rule of heaven is like a thing of great value hidden in a field which someone found and hid (again); then in (delirious) joy he goes and sells everything he owns and buys the whole field. In the same way, the rule of heaven is like a traveling salesman in search of expensive pearls; when he discovers one of inestimable value, he sells everything in order to buy it. (Thomas 109, 76)

13:57b (see Mark 6:4) (Thomas 31)

15:10b-11 (see Mark 7:14b-15) (Thomas 14)

15:14b If a blind person leads another who is blind, eventually both will fall into a ditch. (Quelle)

18: 12-13 What do you think? If a shepherd has a hundred sheep and one of them has wandered off, will he not leave the 99 on the mountains and go in search of the wanderer? And if he finds it, in truth I tell you he rejoices over it more than the 99 that didn't wander off. (Thomas 107 and Quelle)

18:23-33 The rule of heaven may be compared to a king who wanted to settle accounts with his slaves. When he began to figure it out one of them who owed him the equivalent of 15 years' wages was brought to him, and as he was unable to pay his bill, the ruler ordered him to be sold together with his wife and children and all he owned in order to satisfy the bill. Thereupon the slave fell on his knees in front of him, saying, "Have patience with me, and I will pay it all back." Out of compassion, the ruler let him go and forgave the debt. But that same slave, as he left, happened upon one of his fellow slaves who owed him the equivalent of 100 days' wages. He grabbed him around the neck and said, "Pay me what you owe." Thereupon his fellow slave got down on his knees and pleaded with him, "Have patience with me, and I will pay it all back." But he refused and then went and threw him in prison until he would pay the bill. When their fellow slaves saw what had occurred, they were distressed; they went directly to the ruler and reported the whole story. Then the ruler sent for him and said, "You terrible slave. I forgave your debt because you begged me to. Should you not have done as much for your fellow slave?"

19:12 There are eunuchs who have been that way from birth, and there are those who have been made eunuchs by others, and there are eunuchs who have made themselves eunuchs for the sake of the rule of heaven.

19:14 (see Mark 10:14b) (Thomas 22)

19:23-24 (see Mark 10:25)

20:1-16 The rule of heaven is like a landowner who went out first thing in the morning to hire workers for his vineyard. After agreeing with the hires for the customary daily wage of a denarius, he sent them into the vineyard. When he came back around 9 o'clock he saw others standing around doing nothing in the marketplace, and he said to them, "You can have a job, too. Go, and I will pay you whatever is right. So they went. When he came back again around noon and again around three, the same thing occurred. Around five he came back to find others standing around doing nothing, and he said them, "Why are you standing around here doing nothing all day?" They said, "Because nobody offered us a job." He said to them, "You go also into the vineyard (to work)." When the end of the day came, the owner of the vineyard said to his manager, "Call the workers and give them their pay, beginning with the last and then going to the first." As those who were hired at 5 came, each received the customary daily wage. Now when (those hired at 9) came, they thought they would receive more, but each of them received the customary daily wage. And when they received it, they complained to the owner saying, "The last of these worked for only one hour, but you have made them equal with us who have borne the burden during the hottest part of the day." But he answered one of them, "Friend, I have done nothing wrong here; you agreed to work for the usual wage, right? Take it and go; it's yours. It is my choice to give to the last hired what I have given you. Am I not allowed to do what I please with what is mine? Or is your eye envious because I am generous? The last will be first, and the first last." (Thomas 4 and Quelle)

22:1-10 The rule of God is to be compared with a public official who gave a wedding reception for his son. He sent his servants to call those who had been invited, but they said they could not come. So the official sent more messengers with the direction, "Tell those who have invitations, 'See here, the dinner is almost ready ... Come on to the celebration.' But they were unconcerned, and went off, the one to his land, the other to his commerce. ... Then the king told his people that the dinner was ready but those he had invited didn't deserve the invitation, so they should go out into the streets and invite anybody at all to the reception." (Thomas 64 & Quelle)

22:21 (see Mark 12:17) (Thomas 100)

23:5-7 Everything (the scribes and Pharisees) do, they do to be seen. They make their phylacteries broad and their tassels long. (see Mark 12:38-39) (Quelle)

25:14-28 The rule of heaven will be like a man who, going on a journey, summoned his slaves and turned over his money to them; to one he gave the equivalent of 75 years' wages; to another the equivalent of 30 years' wages; to another, 15 years' wages, each according to his ability. Then he left. The one who had gotten 75 years' wages went off and invested them and doubled the amount. Similarly, the one who had gotten 30 years' wages doubled the amount, too. But the fellow with the equivalent of 15 years' wages went off, dug a hole and hid the master's money. After a long time, the slaves' master came back to settle accounts with them. The one who had gotten 75 years' wages brought them and the 75 more, saying, "Master, you gave to me 75 years' wages; see, I have made 75 years' more." His master said to him, "Well done, you good and trustworthy slave; you have been trustworthy in these insignificant things; I will put you in charge of greater matters..." And the one who had gotten 30 years' wages came forth saying, "Master, you gave to me 30 years' wages, see, I have made 30 years' more." His master said to him, "Well done, you good and trustworthy slave. You have been trustworthy in these insignificant things, I will put you in charge of greater things..." Then the one who was given 15 years' wages also came forth, saying, "Master, I knew that you were a harsh man, harvesting where you had not planted and gathering up where you have not scattered seed. Since I was afraid, I went and hid your money in the ground. Here is what belongs to you, (all of it.)" But his master replied, "You terrible and cowardly slave! You knew, did you, that I harvest where I haven't planted and gather up where I have not scattered seed? Then you ought to have invested my funds with the bank so that upon my return I would have received them with interest. So take the money from this slave and give it to the one who now has 150 years' worth of wages." (Quelle)

LUKE

4:24 (see Mark 6:4, Matthew 13:57b) (Thomas 31)

5:31 (see Mark 2:17, Matthew 9:12b)

5:34 (see Mark 2:19, Matthew 9:15)

5:37-39 (see Mark 2:22, Matthew 9:15) (Thomas 47)

6:20b-21 (see Matthew 5:3, 6, 4) (Quelle & Thomas 54)

6:22-23 (See Matthew 5:10-12, Thomas 68, 69 & Quelle)

6:27b (see Matthew 5:44) (Quelle)

6:29, 30 (see Matthew 5:39b - 40, 42) (Quelle and Thomas 95)

6:31 (see Matthew 7:12a, Thomas & Quelle)

6:35 (see Matthew 5:44) (Quelle)

6:37 (see Matthew 6:14) (Quelle)

6:41-42 (see Matthew 7:2b-5) (Thomas 26 & Quelle)

6:44b (see Matthew 7:16b) (Thomas 45 and Quelle)

7:24b-25 (see Matthew 11:7b-8) (Thomas 78 & Quelle)

8:5-8 (see Mark 4:3-8, Matthew 13:3b-8) (Thomas 9)

8:16-17(see Mark 4:21, Matthew 5:15) (Thomas 33, 5 & Quelle)

10:30-35 [It is difficult to include this dear and familiar parable of the good samaritan among Jesus' ethical and wisdom teaching, not because it does not fit with it but because it appears only in Luke, which dates from 85 to 90 C.E. If something so memorable as this parable had been uttered by Jesus, it would surely have been known by Thomas, Mark or Matthew.]

11:2b-4 (see Matthew 6:6, 9, 10a, 11-12, 14-15) (Quelle)

11:9-10(see Matthew 7:7-8) (Thomas 2, 92, 94 and Quelle)

11:24-26 (see Matthew 12: 43-45) (Quelle)

11:33 (see Mark 4:21, Matthew 5:15, Thomas 33 and Quelle)

11:39, 43 (see Mark 12:38, Matthew 23: 5-7, Thomas 89 & Quelle)

123

12:2 (see Mark 10:26, Matthew 10;26) (Thomas 5, 6 and Quelle)

12:17-20 There was a rich man whose fields yielded a big crop. "What should I do?" he asked himself. "Because I do not have sufficient space to store my crop. I know," he said, "I'll raze my barns and put up bigger ones so I can store my grain and other stuff. Then I'll say to myself, 'Self, you have plenty put away for the years to come, so take it easy: eat, drink and indulge yourself.' But God said to him, "You damned fool. Tonight your actual life will be required of you. All that you have accumulated, to whom will it go?" (Thomas 63)

12:22-29 (see Matthew 6:25-31, Thomas 36 & Quelle)

12:58-59(see Matthew 5:25-26) (Quelle)

13:18-19 (see Mark 4:30, Matthew 13:31b-32) (Thomas 20 and Quelle)

13:20 (see Matthew 13:33b) (Thomas 96 and Quelle)

14:16-24 (see Matthew 22: 1-10, Thomas 64 & Quelle)

14:34(see Mark 9:50, Matthew 5:13)

15:11-32 [Here again is one of the most cherished stories in all Hebrew and Christian scriptures, but it appears only in Luke and could not have been kept secret for 50 years until Luke used it. Further, it does not appear to fall into ethical and wisdom teaching but rather seems to have to do with the reconciliation of two related parties who had been separated by conflict or controversy.]

16:1-8a [This parable of the shrewd manager is considered by a number of scholars, including many of the Jesus Seminar, to be an authentic Jesus story. It certainly fits his "economic justice" emphasis, though somewhat obliquely. It has no other parallels even in Thomas, so it is not included here.]

16:13 (see Matthew 6:24) (Thomas 47 and Quelle)

17:20b-21 You will be unable to see the arrival of God's rule.

People won't be able to cry, "Look, here it is!" or "There it is over there!" Rather, God's rule is right there in your midst. (Thomas 133 & Quelle)

18:16 (see Mark 10:14b, Matthew 19:14)

18:24 (see Mark 10:25 and Matthew 19:24)

19:13, 15-24, 26 (see Mark 4:25, Matthew 25:14-30, Thomas 41 and Quelle)

20:25 (see Mark 12:17 and Matthew 22:21) (Thomas 100)

20:46 (see Mark 12:38-39, Matthew 23:5-7) (Quelle)

JOHN

4:44b see Mark 6:4, Matthew 13:57b, Luke 4:24) (Thomas 31)